Addison-Wesley

Algebra

Technology

Created for use with *Addison-Wesley Algebra* Student Text

Stanley A. Smith
Randall I. Charles
John A. Dossey
Mervin L. Keedy
Marvin L. Bittinger

▲▼ **Addison-Wesley Publishing Company**

Menlo Park, California · Reading, Massachusetts · New York
Don Mills, Ontario · Wokingham, England
Amsterdam · Bonn · Sydney · Singapore · Tokyo
Madrid · San Juan

CONTRIBUTING WRITERS

CALCULATOR WORKSHEETS
ROBERT L. REID

SPREADSHEET ACTIVITIES

DEANE E. ARGANBRIGHT
WHITWORTH COLLEGE, SPOKANE, WASHINGTON

ISBN 0-201-25357-7

CDEFGHIJ-AL-943210

Contents

Contents

Calculator Worksheets

The following 32 blackline masters are calculator worksheets, keyed for use with lessons in the text. Each provides practice in working with calculator features such as its memory, exponent, trigonometry, and statistics functions. There is also an Explore section designed to help students apply their calculator skills in problem-solving situations by discovering patterns and in making decisions based on a series of calculations.

Answers will vary for different calculators because of rounding and number of digits.

You will find these worksheets helpful for reviewing and reinforcing concepts as well as providing a challenge for all of your students.

Getting to Know Your Calculator

An expression like 24 − 3 × 5 may be evaluated differently by different calculators.

Evaluate 24 − 3 × 5 on your calculator: 24 $\boxed{-}$ 3 $\boxed{\times}$ 5 $\boxed{=}$ _____

If you obtain 9 for an answer, your calculator follows the Order of Operations. If you obtain 105 for an answer, your calculator follows left-to-right rules. Since the correct answer is 9, you must use parentheses with a calculator that follows left-to-right rules.

Evaluate 24 − (3 × 5) on your calculator. 24 $\boxed{-}$ $\boxed{(}$ 3 $\boxed{\times}$ 5 $\boxed{)}$ $\boxed{=}$ _____

Both types of calculators should give the answer 9.

PRACTICE

Evaluate each expression. Use parentheses if necessary. Round answers to the nearest thousandth.

1. 94 − 19 × 4 + 38 ÷ 19 _____

2. 258 × 93 − 18,766 _____

3. 191 − 44 × 2.3 _____

4. 18.7 + 58.5 ÷ 15 _____

5. 9.8 − 2.1 × 3.3 + 5.2 _____

6. 633.8 ÷ 72 + 44.98 _____

7. 1 × 2 + 3 × 4 + 5 × 6 + 7 × 8 _____

8. 19 − 27 ÷ 18 − 3.5 × 2.2 + 8 ÷ 2.3 _____

EXPLORE

Your calculator has some features you may not be familiar with. The following exercises will help you understand some of those features better.

Your calculator may have two different clear keys: $\boxed{\text{AC/ON}}$ and $\boxed{\text{CE/C}}$. These keys have different functions.

9. Enter 88 $\boxed{+}$ 89 $\boxed{\text{AC/ON}}$ $\boxed{=}$ _____

10. Enter 88 $\boxed{+}$ 89 $\boxed{\text{CE/C}}$ $\boxed{=}$ _____

11. Enter 88 $\boxed{+}$ 89 $\boxed{\text{CE/C}}$ 2 $\boxed{=}$ _____

$\boxed{\text{AC/ON}}$ erases everything you have entered and everything in the calculator's memory. It is equivalent to turning the calculator off and on again. Pressing $\boxed{\text{CE/C}}$ immediately after entering a number erases that number without affecting previously entered numbers or operations. You can use this key when you enter the wrong number by accident.

Different calculators will allow you to enter different numbers of digits.

12. Enter 1,234,567,890. How many digits does your calculator allow you to enter? _____

13. Enter 12,345,678 $\boxed{+}$ 0.12345678 $\boxed{=}$ _____. (You can enter decimal numbers without entering 0 before the decimal point, but it is a good idea to enter a 0 anyway as a reminder to yourself.)

Your calculator probably will not display more than 10 digits. But it may store more than 10.

14. To see how many digits your calculator stores, do not clear the calculation above and enter $\boxed{-}$ 12,345,678 $\boxed{=}$ _____. How many digits does your calculator store? _____

Some calculators will round numbers when they have stored more numbers than are displayed.

15. Enter 11,111,111 $\boxed{+}$ 0.9 _____. Does your calculator round? _____

Exponents

To raise a number to a power on a calculator, use the $\boxed{y^x}$ key.

EXAMPLE   Evaluate 6.8^5.

$$6.8 \quad \boxed{y^x} \quad 5 \quad \boxed{=} \quad \text{14539.33568}$$

When squaring a number you can use the $\boxed{x^2}$ key.

EXAMPLE   Evaluate 14.7^2.

$$14.7 \quad \boxed{x^2} \quad \text{216.09}$$

PRACTICE

Evaluate. Round to the nearest thousandth.

1. 2^{10} _____

2. 88^2 _____

3. 4.1^3 _____

4. 0.53^2 _____

5. 15^6 _____

6. 2.94^4 _____

7. 888^2 _____

8. 277^1 _____

9. $2.2^5 - 1.6^4$ _____

10. $19.5^3 + 6.4^2 \times 1.27^{17}$ _____

EXPLORE

A piece of newspaper 0.0019 inch in thickness is folded in half 25 times. The thickness of the resulting wad of paper is

$$0.0019 \times \underbrace{2 \times 2 \times 2 \times \ldots \times 2}_{25 \text{ times}} = 0.0019 \times 2^{25} \text{ in.}$$

11. Find the thickness in inches.   _____

12. There are 5280 feet in a mile and 12 inches in a foot. Find the number of inches in a mile.   _____

13. Find the thickness of the folded paper in miles. Round to the nearest thousandth.   _____

14. Mr. and Mrs. Ebenezer Smith came to America on the *Mayflower* in 1620. They had 3 children, the first generation of Smiths born in America. Each of these children also had 3 children, the second generation of Smiths. Every Smith thereafter also had 3 children. On July 4, 1988, the 16th generation of Smiths had a family reunion. How many Smiths attended?

_____

Calculate.

15. $(1.01)^{100}$ _____

16. 1^{100} _____

17. $(0.99)^{100}$ _____

18. Does raising a number to a power always make the number larger? Explain.   _____

CALCULATOR WORKSHEET 3

For use with Lesson 1-4

NAME _____

DATE _____

Evaluating Expressions

Because the fraction bar is a grouping symbol, you must calculate the numerator first and then divide by the denominator. Your calculator does this automatically when you use the $\boxed{(}$ and $\boxed{)}$ keys.

EXAMPLE   Evaluate $\frac{9 + 5 \times 3}{2^2}$.

$\boxed{(}$ 9 $\boxed{+}$ 5 $\boxed{\times}$ 3 $\boxed{)}$ $\boxed{\div}$ 2 $\boxed{y^x}$ 2 $\boxed{=}$ $\boldsymbol{\mathsf{6}}$

Omission of the parentheses gives 12.75, an incorrect answer.

PRACTICE

Calculate. Round to the nearest thousandth.

1. $\dfrac{8^3}{4^3}$ _____

2. $\dfrac{6.2^5 - 4.5^4}{8.8^3}$ _____

3. $26 - \dfrac{19.25}{3.5}$ _____

4. $\dfrac{10^2 + 9^2 + 8^2}{7^2}$ _____

5. $5x + 3y$ for $x = 8.8$ and $y = 12.7$ _____

6. $\dfrac{3m - n}{18}$ for $m = 161.9$ and $n = 86.1$ _____

7. $\dfrac{8}{15} - \dfrac{x}{y}$ for $x = 5$ and $y = 17$ _____

8. $f^3 - h^4$ for $f = 1.77$ and $h = 1.18$ _____

9. $374 \div (122 + 119)$ _____

10. $1079 - (1066 - 1043) - (1029 - 1017)$ ____

11. $\dfrac{3371}{8.8 - 6.2}$ _____

12. $400.7 - \left(\dfrac{65}{2.2} - \dfrac{0.9}{13}\right)$ _____

13. $x - (y - z)$ for $x = 816$, $y = 1044$, and $z = 628.7$ _____

EXPLORE

When evaluating expressions containing multiple parentheses, be sure to press a parenthesis key each time a parenthesis symbol appears in the expression. Calculate. Round to the nearest thousandth.

14. $20 - (16 \times (3 - 1.8))$ _____

15. $(462 \times (81 - 19)) - (36 \div (12.5 - 5.7))$ _____

16. $50.2 - (49.3 - (48.4 - (47.5 - 29.7)))$ _____

Calculators can only handle a limited number of pending operations.

17. Enter $10 + (9 - (8 + (7 - (6 + (5 - (4 + 3))))))$. How many left parentheses were you able to enter before you received an error message?

_____ Your calculator cannot handle more than this number of operations at the same time.

Using Memory with Formulas

When you plan to use a number several times in your calculations, store the number in your calculator's memory by pressing $\boxed{\text{STO}}$. Then when you need it, simply press the recall key $\boxed{\text{RCL}}$. (On some calculators, these keys may be labelled $\boxed{\text{M}}$ and $\boxed{\text{MR}}$ for memory and memory recall.)

EXAMPLE   Evaluate $a^2 + 2a + 5$ for $a = 12.79$.
Because we will be using 12.79 twice, we store it in the memory: 12.79 $\boxed{\text{STO}}$.

$\boxed{\text{RCL}}$ $\boxed{x^2}$ $\boxed{+}$ 2 $\boxed{\times}$ $\boxed{\text{RCL}}$ $\boxed{+}$ 5 $\boxed{=}$ **194.1641**

To store a new number, display the number and then press $\boxed{\text{STO}}$.
To clear the memory, display 0 and then press $\boxed{\text{STO}}$, or press $\boxed{\text{AC/ON}}$.

PRACTICE

Evaluate. Round to the nearest thousandth.

1. $y^2 + 13y$ for $y = 0.873$ _____

2. $v^5 - 9v$ for $v = 3.61$ _____

3. $5x^2 - 28x - 17$ for $x = 37.29$ _____

4. $9.8e^5 - 32e^3 + 28.5e$ for $e = 2.337$ _____

EXPLORE

Fleeceville merchants charge a sales tax of 8.2%. The formula for the amount of tax (T) on an item costing D dollars is $T = 0.082D$. Store 0.082 in memory. Then calculate the sales tax on each of the following items. Round to the nearest cent.

5. A $32.98 sweater _____

6. A 39¢ ballpoint pen _____

7. A $23,709 car _____

8. A $1116.29 glockenspiel _____

To add a number to the number already in memory, display the new number and then press $\boxed{\text{SUM}}$.

EXAMPLE   Charlie worked 5 hours at $6.75/hr and 8 hours at $8.15/hr. How much did he earn altogether?

5 $\boxed{\times}$ 6.75 $\boxed{=}$ $\boxed{\text{STO}}$ 8 $\boxed{\times}$ 8.15 $\boxed{=}$ $\boxed{\text{SUM}}$ $\boxed{\text{RCL}}$ **98.95**

He earned $98.95.

The odometer on Etta's car read 45,216.7 miles. Store this number in the memory. Then add the lengths of each of the following trips and give the accumulated odometer reading after each trip.

9. Etta made a 602.9–mile journey to visit her aunt.   _____

10. The first day of her trip home Etta drove 6.25 hr at 52 mph ($d = rt$).   _____

11. She reached home the following day after driving at an average rate of 58.4 mph for 4.75 hr.   _____

12. The following week Etta made 5 round trips to work, driving 11.7 mi each way.   _____

Rational Numbers

To convert a rational number to a decimal, divide the numerator by the denominator.

EXAMPLE   Convert $\frac{17}{25}$ to a decimal.

17 ÷ 25 = 0.68

PRACTICE

Convert to a decimal.

1. $\frac{1}{5}$ _____

2. $4\frac{7}{8}$ _____

3. $\frac{351}{468}$ _____

4. $\frac{1023}{1488}$ _____

5. $\frac{1037}{68}$ _____

6. $22\frac{99}{110}$ _____

7. $\frac{387}{1032}$ _____

8. $\frac{1}{5000}$ _____

EXPLORE

Convert the fractions to decimals and then compare. Use either $<$ or $>$ to write a true sentence.

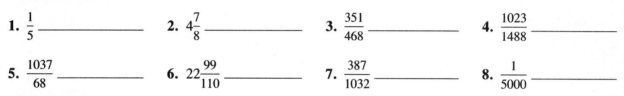

9. $\frac{136}{425}$ = _____

   $\frac{57}{190}$ = _____

   $\frac{136}{425}$ __?__ $\frac{57}{190}$

10. $\frac{91}{650}$ = _____

   $\frac{51}{340}$ = _____

   $\frac{91}{650}$ __?__ $\frac{51}{340}$

11. $\frac{87}{464}$ = _____

   $\frac{527}{2635}$ = _____

   $\frac{87}{464}$ __?__ $\frac{527}{2635}$

Certain denominators have very interesting qualities. Convert to decimals to determine what these qualities are.

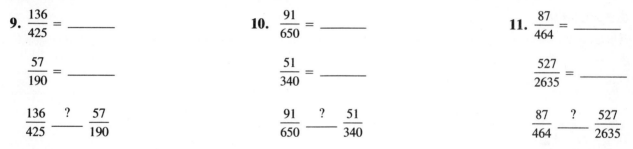

12. $\frac{1}{9}$ = _____

13. $\frac{4}{9}$ = _____

14. $\frac{300}{9}$ = _____

15. $\frac{8}{11}$ = _____

16. $\frac{7}{11}$ = _____

17. $\frac{200}{11}$ = _____

18. $\frac{13}{99}$ = _____

19. $\frac{41}{99}$ = _____

20. $\frac{50}{99}$ = _____

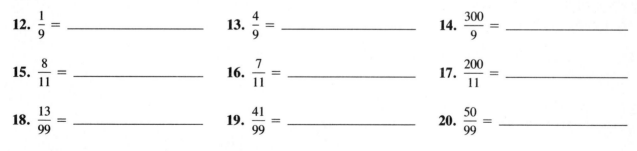

21. Choose some additional fractions with 9, 11, or 99 in their denominators. Convert each to a decimal. Why do some of the conversions show an apparent error in the final digit? _____

Investigate what happens when you convert fractions with only 9's in their denominators to decimals. (Try $\frac{731}{999}$, $\frac{2641}{9999}$, and $\frac{18352}{99999}$, for example.) Then answer the following questions.

22. State a rule about the decimal equivalents of fractions with denominators that consist exclusively of 9's _____

23. Find fractions that convert to the decimals 0.1051051 and 0.8642864. _____

NAME _____

DATE _____

Adding and Subtracting Rational Numbers

You can use the change-sign key $\boxed{+/-}$ to enter negative numbers on your calculator. You must press the key *after* you press the number whose sign you wish to change.

EXAMPLES Calculate $15 + (-3)$.   Calculate $8 - (-13)$.

15 $\boxed{+}$ 3 $\boxed{+/-}$ $\boxed{=}$ **12**   8 $\boxed{-}$ 13 $\boxed{+/-}$ $\boxed{=}$ **21**

PRACTICE
Calculate.

1. $16 + (-73)$ _____

2. $-38 - 112 + (-64)$ _____

3. $997 - (-248) - 761$ _____

4. $143.6 + 811.9 - (-338.5)$ _____

5. $0.709 - (-1.417) + 0.884$ _____

6. $-385 - 447 + 626 + (-791)$ _____

7. $91.3 - (47.2 - 61.6) - (-26 - 39)$ _____

8. $-\dfrac{1}{4} - (-\dfrac{7}{8})$ _____

EXPLORE

The associative property for addition says that when numbers are added, they can be grouped in any order. Is there an associative property for subtraction? To find out, consider the numbers 31.6, -58.1, and 14.9.

9. Evaluate $(31.6 - (-58.1)) - 14.9$. _____

10. Evaluate $31.6 - (-58.1 - 14.9)$. _____

11. When subtracting, does the answer depend on the order in which the numbers are grouped? _____

12. Is there an associative property for subtraction? _____

13. Complete the table, putting information about yourself in the last column.

	Elvis Presley	Napoleon Bonaparte	Martin Luther King	Abraham Lincoln	You
Year of Birth	1935	1769	1929	1809	
Reverse Digits	5391				
Subtract	-3456				
Reverse Digits	-6543				
Add	-9999				

14. Try different birth years to see if the results are always the same. _____

Terminating and Repeating Decimals

Any rational number can be expressed as either a "terminating" decimal (one that ends) or as a repeating decimal. By dividing, you can find the terminating or repeating decimal equivalent of a fraction.

EXAMPLES Write $\frac{16}{625}$ and $\frac{13}{75}$ as terminating or repeating decimals.

$\frac{16}{625} \longrightarrow$ 16 $\boxed{\div}$ 625 $\boxed{=}$ 0.0256 This decimal terminates.

$\frac{13}{75} \longrightarrow$ 13 $\boxed{\div}$ 75 $\boxed{=}$ 0.173333333 This decimal repeats.

Use a bar to indicate which digits repeat: $0.17\overline{3}$

PRACTICE

Write as a decimal. Tell whether the decimal terminates or repeats.

1. $\frac{4}{9}$ _____

2. $\frac{63}{125}$ _____

3. $\frac{39}{520}$ _____

4. $\frac{266497}{1065988}$ _____

5. $\frac{17}{33}$ _____

6. $\frac{169}{2000}$ _____

EXPLORE

The decimal expression for $\frac{1}{7}$ is $0.\overline{142857}$. Store 0.142857 in your calculator's memory.

7. $0.142857 \times 2 =$ _____

8. $0.142857 \times 3 =$ _____

9. $0.142857 \times 4 =$ _____

10. $0.142857 \times 5 =$ _____

11. What peculiarity do you notice about these products? _____

12. Multiply 0.142857×7. _____

13. Divide $\frac{1}{7}$ then multiply this answer times 7. _____

Is this answer the same as the answer for 12? _____

Repeating decimals can be converted to fractions.

EXAMPLE Convert $0.\overline{435}$ to a fraction.

Write an equation.

Count the number of digits that repeat and multiply by 10 raised to that power.

Subtract the first equation.

$n = 0.\overline{435}$

$1000n = 435.\overline{435}$ $(10^3 = 1000)$

$\underline{-\quad n = \quad 0.\overline{435}}$

$999n = 435$

Solve and simplify.

$n = \frac{435}{999} = \frac{145}{333}$

Check by dividing: 145 $\boxed{\div}$ 333 $\boxed{=}$ 0.4354354

Convert to a fraction.

14. $0.\overline{2}$ _____

15. $0.\overline{27}$ _____

16. $0.\overline{83}$ _____

17. $0.\overline{591}$ _____

Reciprocals

By pressing the reciprocal key $\boxed{1/x}$, you can find the reciprocal of the number x.

EXAMPLES **1.** Find the reciprocal of -3.2.

3.2 $\boxed{+/-}$ $\boxed{1/x}$ -0.3125 The reciprocal is -0.3125.

2. Solve $24x = 384$ for x.

384 $\boxed{\times}$ 24 $\boxed{1/x}$ $\boxed{=}$ 16 $x = 16$

PRACTICE

Find the reciprocal.

1. 8 _____

2. 0.001 _____

3. -400 _____

4. $1.\overline{3}$ _____

5. -14.285714 _____

6. 0.375 _____

Solve.

7. $11x = 154$ _____

8. $-31.5k = 11.025$ _____

9. $7603.2 = 576m$ _____

10. $-7.83 = 90p$ _____

EXPLORE

Display 0 on your calculator.

11. Press $\boxed{1/x}$. Explain the result. _____

12. Choose several non-zero numbers. For each number, display the number, then press $\boxed{1/x}$ twice. What happens after $\boxed{1/x}$ is pressed the second time? _____

13. Based on the above results, complete this statement: The reciprocal of the reciprocal of x is _____

14. Suppose you displayed 2 on your calculator, then pressed the reciprocal key 2517 times. What would be the final result? _____

15. There are two numbers that are their own reciprocals. Find them and check your answers on your calculator. _____

Suppose you wanted to find $\frac{4368}{56}$ on your calculator. There are two ways to proceed. You could divide 4368 by 56, or you could multiply 4368 by the reciprocal of 56.

16. Divide 4368 by 56 (4368 $\boxed{\div}$ 56 $\boxed{=}$?). _____

17. Multiply 4368 by the reciprocal of 56 (4368 $\boxed{\times}$ 56 $\boxed{1/x}$ $\boxed{=}$?). _____

18. Which method do you think is better? Why? _____

Evaluating Formulas

Formulas can be evaluated directly by substitution when the desired variable stands alone on one side of the equation.

EXAMPLE $d = rt$ Find d when $r = 330.6$ mi/h and $t = 3.75\ h.$

$$330.6 \boxed{\times} 3.75 \boxed{=} \ \textbf{1239.75}$$

The distance is 1239.75 mi.

When the desired variable does not stand alone, use the addition and multiplication properties to first solve for the variable.

EXAMPLE $A = bh$ Find h when $A = 123.2$ in.^{2} and $b = 22.4$ in.

$$\frac{1}{b} \cdot A = \frac{1}{b} \cdot bh \qquad \text{Solving for } h$$

$$\frac{A}{b} = h$$

$$\frac{123.2}{22.4} = h \qquad \text{Substituting for the variables}$$

$$5.5 = h \qquad 123.4 \boxed{\div} 22.4 \boxed{=} \ \textbf{5.5}$$

The height is 5.5 in.

PRACTICE

Solve.

1. $A = bh$ Find A when $b = 44.6$ cm and $h = 12.5$ cm. _____

2. $d = rt$ Find t when $d = 1337.6$ km and $r = 88$ km/h. _____

3. $P = 2l + 2w$ Find P when $l = 126.5$ yd and $w = 94.7$ yd. _____

4. $I = Prt$ Find r when $I = \$2737$, $P = \$4600$, and $t = 7$ yr. _____

EXPLORE

The $\boxed{\text{2nd}}$ key on your calculator allows you to use the functions printed in small letters above the keys. (This key may also be labelled $\boxed{\text{INV}}$.) An approximation of the number π should be stored on your calculator.

5. Locate π on your calculator and find its approximate value. _____

6. The formula for the area of a circle is $A = \pi r^2$. Use the value of π given by your calculator and the $\boxed{x^2}$ key to find the area of a circle to the nearest hundredth with radius $r = 8.7$ in. _____

7. The formula for the circumference of a circle is $C = 2\pi r$. Find the radius of a circle to the nearest hundredth whose circumference is 60 in. _____

Proportions

Use the multiplication property to solve proportions on a calculator.

EXAMPLES **1.** Solve $\dfrac{x}{24} = \dfrac{66}{132}$.

$$24 \cdot \dfrac{x}{24} = 24 \cdot \dfrac{66}{132}$$

$$x = 24 \;\boxed{\times}\; 66 \;\boxed{\div}\; 132 \;\boxed{=}\; \text{12} \qquad x = 12$$

2. Solve $\dfrac{94}{15} = \dfrac{1222}{y}$.

$$15y \cdot \dfrac{94}{15} = 15y \cdot \dfrac{1222}{y}$$

$$94y = 15 \cdot 1222$$

$$\dfrac{1}{94} \cdot 94y = \dfrac{1}{94} \cdot 15 \cdot 1222$$

$$y = 94 \;\boxed{1/x}\; \boxed{\times}\; 15 \;\boxed{\times}\; 1222 \;\boxed{=}\; \text{195} \qquad y = 195$$

PRACTICE

Solve.

1. $\dfrac{144}{54} = \dfrac{x}{99}$ $\quad x =$ _____

2. $\dfrac{8.1}{12.6} = \dfrac{24.3}{m}$ $\quad m =$ _____

3. $\dfrac{k}{1.5} = \dfrac{2.2}{1.65}$ $\quad k =$ _____

4. $\dfrac{990}{p} = \dfrac{5.61}{0.85}$ $\quad p =$ _____

5. $\dfrac{61.2}{9} = \dfrac{r}{43.2}$ $\quad r =$ _____

6. $\dfrac{0.77}{0.028} = \dfrac{2.541}{h}$ $\quad h =$ _____

EXPLORE

A quick way to check if a proportion is true is to multiply each numerator by the opposite denominator. If the products are equal, the proportion is true.

EXAMPLE $\dfrac{9}{75} \overset{?}{=} \dfrac{14.4}{120}$

$$9 \;\boxed{\times}\; 120 \;\boxed{=}\; \text{1080} \qquad 75 \;\boxed{\times}\; 14.4 \;\boxed{=}\; \text{1080}$$

The products are equal, so the proportion checks.

Write "Yes" if the proportion is true. Otherwise write "No."

7. $\dfrac{8}{21} = \dfrac{232}{609}$ _____

8. $\dfrac{512}{125} = \dfrac{64}{15.625}$ _____

9. $\dfrac{364.5}{256} = \dfrac{1458}{1024}$ _____

10. $\dfrac{0.94}{0.016} = \dfrac{1.18}{0.02}$ _____

11. $\dfrac{147}{192.5} = \dfrac{42}{55}$ _____

12. $\dfrac{68}{89} = \dfrac{646}{846}$ _____

Using Percent

The % function on your calculator allows you to determine percents easily.

EXAMPLES   **1.** Express $\frac{7}{8}$ as a percent.

$$7 \boxed{\div} 8 \boxed{\%} \boxed{=} \quad 87.5 \qquad \frac{7}{8} = 87.5\%$$

2. 125% of what number is 184?

$$184 \boxed{\div} 125 \boxed{\%} \boxed{=} \quad 147.2 \qquad 125\% \text{ of } 147.2 = 184$$

PRACTICE

Express as a percent. Round to the nearest tenth of a percent.

1. $\frac{21}{112}$ _____   **2.** $\frac{347}{476}$ _____   **3.** $\frac{264}{165}$ _____

Solve.

4. 84% of 632 is what number? _____   **5.** What percent of 4000 is 3664? _____

6. What is 26.5% of $172? _____   **7.** 350% of what number is 1995? _____

EXPLORE

Percent price increases or decreases are easy to calculate.

EXAMPLES   **1.** A $48 blouse was marked down 30%. Find the sale price.

$$48 \boxed{-} 30 \boxed{\%} \boxed{=} \quad 33.6 \qquad \text{The sale price was } \$33.60.$$

2. 4.5% sales tax was added to the above price.   Find the total cost.

$$33.60 \boxed{+} 4.5 \boxed{\%} \boxed{=} \quad 35.112 \qquad \text{The cost rounds to } \$35.11.$$

Solve.

8. During an inventory sale all musical instruments were marked down 45%. Find the sale price of an $860 saxophone. _____

9. The price of a $27.50 telephone rose 8%. If 6% sales tax is added to the price, how much will the phone cost? _____

10. Megan's salary in 1985 was $22,000. She received a 5% pay increase in 1986, 1987, and 1988. What was her 1988 salary? _____

The price of an item went up 10%. A month later it went down 10%.

11. Is the price more than, less than, or the same as it was before? _____

12. To check your answer, take a specific example such as a $400 television set. Increase the price by 10%, then decrease the *new* price by 10%. Compare the final price with the original. _____

Repeated Operations

Many calculators allow you to store a number and an operation for repeated use.

EXAMPLE Halley's Comet appears every 76 years. It most recently appeared in 1986. Find the dates of its five previous appearances.

First program the calculator to subtract 76 repeatedly.

76 $\boxed{-}$ $\boxed{=}$ **0**

(If your calculator has a $\boxed{K}$ key, you must press $\boxed{K}$ before you press $\boxed{=}$.)

Now, each time you press $\boxed{=}$, 76 will be subtracted from the number in the display.

1986 $\boxed{=}$ **1910** $\boxed{=}$ **1834** $\boxed{=}$ **1758** $\boxed{=}$ **1682** $\boxed{=}$ **1606**

You can also program the calculator to add a number repeatedly (n $\boxed{+}$ $\boxed{=}$), to multiply or divide by a number repeatedly (n $\boxed{\times}$ $\boxed{=}$ or n $\boxed{\div}$ $\boxed{=}$), and to raise to a certain power repeatedly (n $\boxed{y^x}$ $\boxed{=}$). Note that as soon as you enter another operation or clear the calculator, the programmed function is erased from the memory.

PRACTICE

1. Carl saves $145 per month. Currently he has $2652 in his savings account. How much will he have at the end of each of the next five months? _____

2. Each new generation of lemmings is six times as large as the last. There are currently 42 lemmings. How many will there be in each of the next five generations? _____

3. Each higher setting on a microscope reduces the area of a slide observed by a factor of 3.2. The number of cells that can be observed at one setting is 33,554,432. How many can be observed at each of the next five higher settings? _____

EXPLORE

Program your calculator to multiply by 26.7. Then test each of the following values of x to see which satisfy the inequality $26.7x < 138.84$. Answer "Yes" or "No."

4. $x = 5$ _____ 5. $x = 5.3$ _____ 6. $x = 5.18$ _____ 7. $x = 5.2$ _____

Program your calculator to raise to the 5th power. Then test each of the following values of x to see which satisfy the inequality $x^5 < 9$. Answer "Yes" or "No."

8. $x = 1.3$ _____ 9. $x = 1.55$ _____ 10. $x = 1.56$ _____ 11. $x = 1.552$ _____

12. Find a multiple of 119 less than 2000 that contains three 6's in a row. (Hint: Program your calculator to add 119 repeatedly. Press $\boxed{=}$ to find successive multiples of 119.) _____

13. Find a multiple of 753 less than 10,000 that contains three 7's in a row. _____

Working with Exponents

Use the $\boxed{y^x}$ key to raise a number to a power.

EXAMPLE Find $(8.5)^4$.

$$8.5 \;\boxed{y^x}\; 4 \;\boxed{=}\; \mathsf{5220.0625}$$

EXAMPLE Find $(0.01)^{-3}$.

$$.01 \;\boxed{y^x}\; 3 \;\boxed{+/-}\; \boxed{=}\; \mathsf{1000000}$$

PRACTICE

Evaluate. Round to the nearest thousandth.

1. 5^5 _____

2. $(1.2)^9$ _____

3. $(0.2^2)^{-2}$ _____

4. $(7.2 \times 3.1)^4$ _____

5. $\left(\dfrac{160}{5.5}\right)^3$ _____

6. $3^5 \cdot 2^{-5}$ _____

7. $\left(\dfrac{28.3}{29.1}\right)^{15}$ _____

8. $(3^4 + 2^6)^3$ _____

EXPLORE

9. Program your calculator to multiply -1 by itself repeatedly.
$(1 \;\boxed{+/-}\; \boxed{\times}\; \boxed{K}\;)$ Now press $\boxed{=}$ several times. Tell what
happens and explain the result. _____

10. What is $(-1)^7$? $(-1)^{11}$? $(-1)^{19}$? _____

11. A negative number is used as a factor an even number of times. Is
the result positive or negative? _____

Some calculators will not calculate powers of negative numbers. Determine if yours does by entering
$2 \;\boxed{+/-}\; \boxed{y^x}\; 3$. If you received an error message, you must find the same power of the absolute value
of the number and then affix the correct sign.

Evaluate.

12. $(-2)^{16}$ _____

13. $(-7)^5$ _____

14. $(-0.032)^{-3}$ _____

Many numbers can be expressed using three 2's.

$$2 + 2 + 2 = 6 \qquad 2 \times 2 \times 2 = 8 \qquad (2)^{2 \times 2} = 16 \qquad 222 = 222$$

15. What is the largest number you can find that can be expressed
using three 2's? _____

16. What is the smallest positive number you can find that can be
expressed using three 2's and a minus sign? _____

Using Scientific Notation

Most calculators cannot display numbers larger than 9,999,999,999 in standard notation. Larger numbers are displayed using scientific notation.

EXAMPLE Find 2^{40}. 2 $\boxed{y^x}$ 40 $\boxed{=}$ `1.099511628  12`

The 12 indicates the power of 10 in scientific notation.

$$2^{40} = 1.099511628 \times 10^{12}$$

The $\boxed{\text{EXP}}$ key (on some calculators it is labelled $\boxed{\text{EE}}$) allows you to enter numbers in scientific notation.

EXAMPLE Enter 5.7061×10^{23} 5.7061 $\boxed{\text{EXP}}$ 23

PRACTICE

Evaluate. Write answers using scientific notation.

1. 5^{23} _____

2. $(0.02)^{33}$ _____

3. 17^{-8} _____

4. $(-456)^{27}$ _____

5. $(6.3384 \times 10^{49}) \times (2.55 \times 10^{-11})$ _____

6. $2^3 \times 4^5 \times 6^7$ _____

7. $(8.33 + 6.57^3)^8$ _____

EXPLORE

8. What is the largest number that you can express on your calculator? _____

9. $x!$ means to multiply together all natural numbers up to and including x. $(5! = 5 \cdot 4 \cdot 3 \cdot 2 \cdot 1)$ Many calculators have an $x!$ function. What is the largest number for which you can find $x!$ on your calculator? _____

10. Suppose you live to be 80 years old. If your heart beats 72 times per minute, how many times will it beat in 80 years? (Assume 365.25 days per year.) Express your answer in scientific notation. _____

The United States government spreads about a trillion (1×10^{12}) dollars per year.

11. There are about 250 million citizens of the United States. About how much does the government spend per person? Express your answer in standard notation. _____

12. There are about half a million minutes in one year. About how much does the government spend each minute? Express your answer in standard notation. _____

Evaluating Polynomials

Use the calculator's memory keys (| STO | and | RCL |) to evaluate polynomials more efficiently.

EXAMPLE Evaluate $x^4 + 2x^2 - 5$ for $x = 2.6$.

First store $x = 2.6$ in memory: 2.6 | STO |

| RCL | y^x 4 | + | 2 | × | | RCL | y^x 2 | − | 5 | = | 54.2176

PRACTICE

Evaluate each polynomial for the given value. Round answers to the nearest thousandth.

1. $x^2 - x - 56$ for $x = 8$ _____

2. $3(x^3 + x^2 + x + 1)$ for $x = 4$ _____

3. $5x^2 - 10x - 12$ for $x = 24$ _____

4. $x^5 + x^4 - x^3 + x^2 - 1$ for $x = 7$ _____

5. $-26x^3 + 19x^2 + 32x$ for $x = 2.16$ _____

6. $18x^{10} - 9x^5 + 3x^2 - 42$ for $x = 1.73$ _____

EXPLORE

A ball is thrown vertically upward at a velocity of 80 ft/sec. Its distance above the ground after t seconds is given by the formula $d = -16t^2 + 80t$. Find the ball's height after each of the following elapsed times.

7. 0.755 _____

8. 1.55 _____

9. 2.55 _____

10. Find the ball's height 2 seconds after it is thrown and 3 seconds after it is thrown. Explain your answer. _____

_____

11. Find the ball's height 5 seconds after it is thrown. Explain your answer. _____

_____

The formula for the area of a circle is $A = \pi r^2$. The formula for the surface area of a sphere is $S = 4\pi r^2$. The formula for the volume of a sphere is $V = \frac{4}{3}\pi r^3$. Assume the circle and the sphere each has a radius of 8.4 cm. Store 8.4 in memory and then find the following using the value of π given by your calculator. Round answers to the nearest thousandth.

12. Area of circle _____

13. Surface area of sphere _____

14. Volume of sphere _____

The weekly profit, in dollars, of a doorknob manufacturer is given by the formula $P = 2x - 0.0001x^2 - 250$, where x is the number of doorknobs sold. Find the profit when these quantities of doorknobs are sold.

15. 2000 _____

16. 8000 _____

17. 15,000 _____

18. Does the manufacturer's profit increase with an increase of doorknob sales? _____

Finding Factors

To factor polynomials, you must be able to find factors of the constant term. If the term is small you can easily think of factors. Suppose, however, it is large: $x^2 - 12x - 8613$. The rules of divisibility will help you find the factors of numbers whose factors are not obvious.

Rules of Divisibility	
A number is divisible by . . .	If . . .
2	it is even.
3	the sum of its digits is divisible by 3.
5	it ends in 5 or 0.
9	the sum of its digits is divisible by 9.
11	the sum of the digits in even-numbered positions minus the sum of the digits in odd-numbered positions is zero or a multiple of 11.

EXAMPLE   Test 8613 for divisibility by 11.

The sum of its even-numbered digits $(6 + 3)$ less the sum of its odd-numbered digits $(8 + 1) = 11 - 11 = 0$, so 8613 is divisible by 11.

8613 $\boxed{\div}$ 11 $\boxed{=}$ 783

PRACTICE

Complete the table by testing for divisibility by 2, 3, 5, 9, and 11. Write either "No" or the result of dividing n by 2, 3, 5, 9, or 11.

	n Divisible by:	2?	3?	5?	9?	11?
1.	8613					783
2.	4845					
3.	67,232					
4.	36,630					
5.	19,427					
6.	13,155					
7.	29,337					

EXPLORE

Larger factors can be found by multiplying together smaller factors. For example, since 3685 is divisible by both 5 and 11, it is also divisible by 55(5×11).

3685 $\boxed{\div}$ 55 $\boxed{=}$ 67

For each number, find a factor larger than 11 and tell the result of dividing the given number by the factor.

EXAMPLE $3685 = 55 \times 67$

8. $16,522 =$ _____ $\times$ _____

9. $21,135 =$ _____ $\times$ _____

10. $32,043 =$ _____ $\times$ _____

11. $27,665 =$ _____ $\times$ _____

12. $36,945 =$ _____ $\times$ _____

13. $31,077 =$ _____ $\times$ _____

Checking Solutions of Equations

Is $x = 4.5$ a solution of the equation $x^2 - 4x - 2.25 = 0$?
To find out, store 4.5 in memory: 4.5 [STO]
Now evaluate the polynomial:

[RCL] [x^2] [−] 4 [×] [RCL] [−] 2.25 [=] **0**

The result is 0, so $x = 4.5$ is a solution of the equation.

PRACTICE

Decide if the given value of the variable satisfies the equation. Write "Yes" or "No."

1. $x^2 - 6x - 11.25 = 0$ for $x = 7.5$ _____

2. $v^2 + 23v - 1428 = 0$ for $v = -28$ _____

3. $3x^2 - 42x + 64 = 0$ for $x = 12.25$ _____

4. $-6x^2 - 32x + 14.375 = 0$ for $x = -5.75$ _____

5. $w^3 + 2w^2 + w - 1.5 = 0$ for $w = 0.6$ _____

6. $x^8 - 216x^3 - 729 = 0$ for $x = 3$ _____

EXPLORE

We can decide if a binomial is a factor of a given polynomial by writing an equation.

EXAMPLE   Determine whether $(x - 5)$ is a factor of $x^2 + 17x - 110$.
Set the polynomial equal to 0: $x^2 + 17x - 110 = 0$
Now check to see if the *opposite* of the number in the binomial $(x - 5)$ is a solution to the equation.
The opposite of -5 is 5, so we store 5: 5 [STO]

[RCL] [x^2] [+] 17 [×] [RCL] [−] 110 [=] **0**

The result is 0, so $(x - 5)$ is a factor of $x^2 + 17x - 110$.

Decide if the binomial is a factor of the given polynomial. Write "Yes" or "No."

7. $(x - 6); 4x^2 - 12x - 72$ _____   **8.** $(x + 11); 9x^2 + 89x - 110$ _____

9. $(x - 15.25); 3x^2 - 46.25x + 7.625$ _____

10. $(x + 35); x^2 + 33x - 2380$ _____   **11.** $(x - 7); -3x^4 + 21x^3$ _____

Use the Guess, Check, and Revise problem-solving strategy to solve. All solutions are whole numbers.

12. $x^4 = 83,521$ (Try $x = 15$. Then revise upward or downward
depending on the result.) $x =$ _____

13. $x^8 = 6561$ $x =$ _____   **14.** $x^5 = 9,765,625$ $x =$ _____

15. $x^3 = 238,328$ $x =$ _____   **16.** $x^4 = 923,521$ $x =$ _____

Algebra Technology

Graphing

Drawing up a table of ordered pairs is sometimes made easier by using the constant function.

EXAMPLE Complete the table of ordered pairs
for the equation $y = 8x$.

First program the calculator to multiply by 8:

8 $\boxed{\times}$ $\boxed{=}$ (If your calculator has a $\boxed{K}$ key, press 8 $\boxed{\times}$ $\boxed{K}$.)

Then enter each value of x:

-3 $\boxed{=}$ -24; 5 $\boxed{=}$ 40; 7 $\boxed{=}$ 56; 15 $\boxed{=}$ 120

The numbers -24, 40, 56, and 120 can be entered in the table under y.

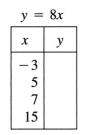

$y = 8x$	
x	y
-3	
5	
7	
15	

PRACTICE

Program the constant function and complete the table for the given equation. **Round to the nearest hundredth.**

1. $y = 12x$

x	y
-6	
-3	
9	
13	

2. $y = -15.5x$

x	y
-9.2	
-6.5	
4.7	
5.2	

3. $y = 0.34x$

x	y
-21	
-16	
3.7	
8.8	

EXPLORE

Determine whether the point lies on the graph of the equation. Answer "Yes" or "No."

4. $(3, 23)$, $y = 14x - 29$ _____

5. $(-2.5, -40)$, $y = 34x + 45$ _____

6. $(25, -27)$, $y = -4.4x + 83$ _____

7. $(63, 11{,}769)$, $y = 3x^2 - 2x - 12$ _____

Determine which points satisfy the equation $x^2 + y^2 = 25$. Answer "Yes" or "No." Plot the points and draw the graph.

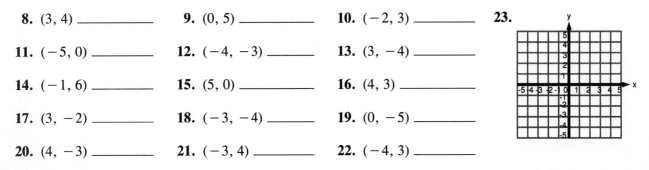

8. $(3, 4)$ _____

9. $(0, 5)$ _____

10. $(-2, 3)$ _____

23.

11. $(-5, 0)$ _____

12. $(-4, -3)$ _____

13. $(3, -4)$ _____

14. $(-1, 6)$ _____

15. $(5, 0)$ _____

16. $(4, 3)$ _____

17. $(3, -2)$ _____

18. $(-3, -4)$ _____

19. $(0, -5)$ _____

20. $(4, -3)$ _____

21. $(-3, 4)$ _____

22. $(-4, 3)$ _____

Systems of Equations

Use of a calculator can make it easier to solve a system of equations.

EXAMPLE   Solve $7x - 13y = 17$
$6x + 5y = 63$

To make the x-terms additive inverses, we can multiply the first equation by -6 and the second by 7.

6 [+/−] [×] [=] This programs the calculator to multiply by -6. (If your calculator has a [K] key, press 6 [+/−] [×] [K] .) We enter the numbers of the first equation:

7 [=] -42 -13 [=] 78 17 [=] -102

Equation 1 becomes: $-42x + 78y = -102$
Similarly we rewrite equation 2: $42x + 35y = 441$
Adding: 78 [+] 35 [=] 113
-102 [+] 441 [=] 339

Dividing: 339 [÷] 113 [=] 3

$113y = 339$

$y = 3$

To find x we substitute $y = 3$ in equation 1:

$7x - 13(3) = 17$ 13 [×] 3 [=] 39
$7x - 39 = 17$
$7x = 17 + 39$ 17 [+] 39 [=] 56
$x = 56 \div 7$ 56 [÷] 7 [=] 8
$x = 8$

The solution of the system is (8, 3).

PRACTICE

Solve.

1. $5x + 2y = -4$ Solution: _____
$-6x + 5y = 27$

2. $8x - 12y = -8$ Solution: _____
$-11x + 10y = -15$

3. $12x - 9y = -30$ Solution: _____
$-17x + 12y = 23$

4. $20x - 24y = 16.4$ Solution: _____
$38x - 15y = 227$

EXPLORE

5. $8x + 4y - 7z = -23$ Use substitution to find z if $x = 21$ and $y = -25$.

_____

The solution of the following system is (8, 13). Find the value of A and B by substituting $x = 8$ and $y = 13$.

6. $Ax - 2y = -2$
$7x - By = 4$

$A = $ _____

$B = $ _____

Rational Equations and Formulas

Many formulas take the form of rational equations. Using the reciprocal key $\boxed{1/x}$ often makes it easier to solve these equations.

EXAMPLE Abbie, Barbara, and Carlos can each plow a field in 8 hours, 7 hours, and 6.75 hours. How long will the job take if they work together?

The time (T) to do a job is related to the time it takes individuals to do the same job (T_1, T_2, T_3 . . .) as follows:

$$\frac{1}{T} = \frac{1}{T_1} + \frac{1}{T_2} + \frac{1}{T_3} + \cdots$$

$$\frac{1}{T} = \frac{1}{8} + \frac{1}{7} + \frac{1}{6.75}$$

$$\frac{1}{T} = 8 \;\boxed{1/x}\quad \boxed{+}\quad 7 \;\boxed{1/x}\quad \boxed{+}\quad 6.75 \;\boxed{1/x}$$

$$= 0.416005291$$

This is $\frac{1}{T}$, so press $\boxed{1/x}$ to find T: 2.40381558. The job will take about 2.4 hours.

PRACTICE

Solve. Round to the nearest tenth.

1. Annabel can prune a wisteria in 45 minutes. Fong can prune the same plant in 38 minutes. How long will it take them working together?   _____

2. Five volunteers are stuffing envelopes for candidate Tweed. Working alone they would require 2.4, 3.5, 2.2, 3.1, and 2.9 hours respectively to do the job. How long will it take them working together?   _____

EXPLORE

3. The resistance of electrical appliances is measured in ohms. The total resistance (R) of several appliances is related to the individual resistances (R_1, R_2, R_3, . . .) by

$$\frac{1}{R} = \frac{1}{R_1} + \frac{1}{R_2} + \frac{1}{R_3} + \cdots$$

Four appliances with resistances of 24, 9, 18, and 32 ohms are plugged into a wall outlet. Find the total resistance.   _____

4. Find the total resistance of 7 appliances having resistances of 14, 9, 26, 35, 42.5, 18.5, and 23.75 ohms.   _____

5. Three appliances have a total resistance of 5.8 ohms. If the resistances of two of the appliances are 15 and 18 ohms respectively, what is the resistance of the third?   _____

Square Roots and Irrational Numbers

To find the square root of a number, use the $\sqrt{x}$ function on your calculator. If the $\sqrt{x}$ function is above the x^2 function, you will need to press [INV] or [2ND] [x^2] .

EXAMPLE   Find $\sqrt{28}$.

28 [$\sqrt{x}$] 5.291502622 $\sqrt{28} \approx 5.291502622$

PRACTICE

Find the square root. Round to the nearest hundredth.

1. $\sqrt{25}$ _____

2. $\sqrt{169}$ _____

3. $-\sqrt{302.76}$ _____

4. $-\sqrt{1.1881}$ _____

5. $\sqrt{7.29 \times 10^{42}}$ _____

6. $\sqrt{10^{16}}$ _____

EXPLORE

The first 10 perfect squares are 1, 4, 9, 16, 25, 36, 49, 64, 81, and 100.

7. Write the next 10 perfect squares.   _____

8. Look at the ones digits of the first 20 perfect squares. From the pattern you observe, predict the ones digit of the next perfect square after 172,225.   _____

9. The ones digit of a certain perfect square is 9. What is the ones digit of the following perfect square?   _____

10. Find a perfect square between 120,000 and 121,000.   _____

Is $\sqrt{A + B} = \sqrt{A} + \sqrt{B}$? To find out, let $A = 100$ and $B = 576$.

11. Find $\sqrt{100 + 576}$. (Use parentheses to find the sum before calculating the square root.) Find $\sqrt{100} + \sqrt{576}$.   _____

12. Does $\sqrt{100 + 576} = \sqrt{100} + \sqrt{576}$?   _____

Simplify.

13. $\sqrt{487 + 957}$ _____

14. $\sqrt{3291 + 1716 + 2218}$ _____

15. $\sqrt{51^2 + 68^2}$ _____

16. $\sqrt{215^2 + 912^2}$ _____

17. In the fifth century, the Chinese astronomer Tsu Ch'ung-Chih discovered a fraction that gives an amazingly close approximation of π. To remember it, write the first three odd integers in pairs:

   1, 1, 3, 3, 5, 5

Now write the last three digits above the first three: $\dfrac{355}{113}$

This is Tsu Ch'ung-Chih's fraction. Find the difference between its decimal equivalent and your calculator's value of π.   _____

Evaluating Radical Expressions

You can use the $\sqrt{x}$ function on a calculator to evaluate radical expressions. The calculator will always find the principal square root.

EXAMPLE Evaluate $\sqrt{57x^2 - y}$ for $x = 14$ and $y = -5$.

$\boxed{(\ }$ 57 $\boxed{\times}$ 14 $\boxed{x^2}$ $\boxed{-}$ 5 $\boxed{+/-}$ $\boxed{)}$ $\boxed{\sqrt{x}}$ **105.7213318**

PRACTICE

Evaluate. Round answers to the nearest thousandth.

1. $\sqrt{x^3 - 9}$ for $x = 22$ _____

2. $\sqrt{x^2 + y^2}$ for $x = 1.9$ and $y = 2.6$ _____

3. $\sqrt{39m^2 - 13m}$ for $m = 13$ _____

4. $\sqrt{y^4 + y^3 + y^2 + y}$ for $y = 13$ _____

EXPLORE

5. Evaluate $\sqrt{32x}$ for $x = -0.5$. Explain the result. _____

6. Evaluate $\sqrt{17.4^2 + 93.96 + 2.7^2}$ and $\sqrt{(17.4 + 2.7)^2}$. Explain the result.

_____

You can use the $\boxed{y^x}$ key to calculate expressions that have fractional exponents.

EXAMPLE Find $5045.589^{1/2}$.

$\qquad$ 5045.589 $\boxed{y^x}$ $\boxed{(\ }$ 1 $\boxed{\div}$ 2 $\boxed{)}$ $\boxed{=}$ **71.03230955**

Calculate.

7. $49^{1/2}$ _____

8. $169^{1/2}$ _____

9. $16^{1/2}$ _____

10. What do you notice? _____

11. Fill in the blank. $\sqrt{x}$ is written as _____ in exponential notation.

12. You know that $\dfrac{1}{x}$ is written in exponential notation as x^{-1}.

How would you write $\dfrac{1}{\sqrt{y}}$ in exponential notation? _____

Calculate.

13. $125^{1/3}$ _____

14. $512^{1/3}$ _____

15. $1331^{1/3}$ _____

16. $4096^{1/4}$ _____

17. $248,832^{1/5}$ _____

18. $5,764,801^{1/8}$ _____

19. Calculate $8^{2/3}$. _____ How can you write $8^{2/3}$ without using fractional exponents? _____

Rational Exponents and Roots

Just as $\sqrt{x} = x^{1/2}$, $\sqrt[3]{x} = x^{1/3}$, $\sqrt[4]{x} = x^{1/4}$, $\sqrt[5]{x} = x^{1/5}$, etc.

EXAMPLE   Simplify. $\sqrt[5]{161051}$

$$\sqrt[5]{161051} = 161051^{1/5}$$

161051 $\boxed{y^x}$ $\boxed{(}$ 1 $\boxed{\div}$ 5 $\boxed{)}$ $\boxed{=}$ **11**

You can express $\sqrt[2]{9^3}$ as $(9^3)^{1/2} = 9^{3/2}$, which can be evaluated by the calculator:

9 $\boxed{y^x}$ $\boxed{(}$ 3 $\boxed{\div}$ 2 $\boxed{)}$ $\boxed{=}$ **27.**

PRACTICE

1. $\sqrt[4]{625}$ _____

2. $\sqrt[2]{10,000}$ _____

3. $\sqrt[5]{1024}$ _____

4. $\sqrt[8]{5,764,801}$ _____

5. $\sqrt[6]{2}$ _____

6. $\sqrt[7]{78,125}$ _____

7. $49^{3/2}$ _____

8. $32^{7/5}$ _____

9. $81^{3/4}$ _____

10. $\sqrt[4]{2401^5}$ _____

11. $\sqrt[4]{50,625^2}$ _____

12. $\sqrt[6]{262,144^5}$ _____

EXPLORE

13. Find the following: $1^2 =$ _____

$11^2 =$ _____

$111^2 =$ _____

$1111^2 =$ _____

14. If you find 1111111^2 on your calculator, the answer will be expressed in scientific notation. Based on the results to Exercise 13, determine the exact number that is equal to 1111111^2. _____

15. Find $\sqrt[3]{\sqrt[5]{14,348,907}}$. (Evaluate the inner radical first, then the outer radical.) _____

16. Find $\sqrt[15]{14,348,907}$. _____

17. Compare your results to Exercises 14 and 15. Based on what you find, solve for x: $\sqrt[7]{\sqrt[9]{171}} = \sqrt[x]{171}$ _____

18. Find $\sqrt[2]{\sqrt[3]{\sqrt[4]{16,777,216}}}$ _____

19. Solve for x:

$$\sqrt[2]{\sqrt[3]{\sqrt[4]{16,777,216}}} = \sqrt[x]{16,777,216}$$ _____

Pythagorean Triples

When the lengths of the sides of a right triangle are whole numbers, the three lengths are called a Pythagorean triple.

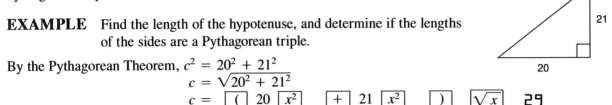

EXAMPLE   Find the length of the hypotenuse, and determine if the lengths of the sides are a Pythagorean triple.

By the Pythagorean Theorem, $c^2 = 20^2 + 21^2$
$$c = \sqrt{20^2 + 21^2}$$
$$c = \boxed{(}\ 20\ \boxed{x^2}\ \boxed{+}\ 21\ \boxed{x^2}\ \boxed{)}\ \boxed{\sqrt{x}}\ \ \text{29}$$

The length of the hypotenuse is 29. The numbers 20, 21, and 29 form a Pythagorean triple as each is a whole number.

PRACTICE

Find the third side of the right triangle. Round to the nearest hundredth. Tell if the lengths form a Pythagorean triple.

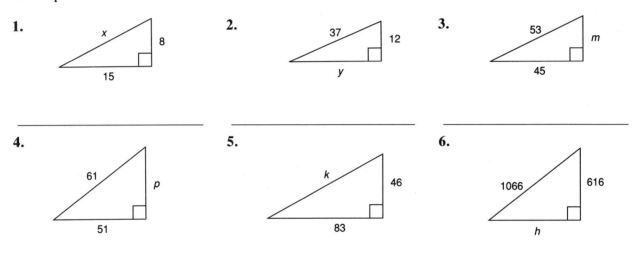

1. x, 8, 15

2. 37, 12, y

3. 53, m, 45

_____   _____   _____

4. 61, p, 51

5. k, 46, 83

6. 1066, 616, h

_____   _____   _____

EXPLORE

By substituting whole number values of p and q in the expressions $a = p^2 - q^2$, $b = 2pq$, and $c = p^2 + q^2$, all Pythagorean triples can be found. The number p must be larger than q. Furthermore, p and q cannot share a common factor, and one must be odd, the other even.

EXAMPLE   Find the Pythagorean triple when $p = 4$ and $q = 3$.

$$a = p^2 - q^2 = 4^2 - 3^2 = 16 - 9 = 7$$
$$b = 2pq = 2(4)(3) = 24$$
$$c = p^2 + q^2 = 4^2 + 3^2 = 16 + 9 = 25$$

The Pythagorean triple is 7, 24, 25. ($7^2 + 24^2 = 49 + 576 = 625 = 25^2$) Find Pythagorean triples for these values of p and q. Check each triple on your calculator.

7. $p = 2, q = 1$ _____   **8.** $p = 7, q = 4$ _____

9. $p = 17, q = 13$ _____   **10.** $p = 31, q = 26$ _____

Evaluating Functions

The memory and the constant function features on your calculator can both be useful in evaluating functions.

EXAMPLES **1.** Evaluate $f(x) = 3x^3 - x^2 - 7x$ for $x = 11.3$.
Store 11.3 in the memory: 11.3 [STO]

3 [×] [RCL] [y^x] 3 [−] [RCL] [x^2] [−] 7

[×] [RCL] [=] `4121.901`

2. Evaluate $f(x) = -5x^2$ for $x = 3$ and $x = 0.75$.
Program the calculator to multiply by -5: 5 [+/−] [×] [=]
(If your calculator has a [K] key, press it before [=] .)
Enter a value for x, press [x^2], and press [=] :

3 [x^2] [=] `-45`   0.75 [x^2] [=] `-2.8125`

PRACTICE

Evaluate. Round to the nearest thousandth.

1. $f(x) = 13x^2 - 6x^3 + 4x$ for $x = 7.21$ _____

2. $f(x) = 1.72x^2$ for $x = 5.7$ _____ $x = 0.6$ _____ $x = -9.1$ _____

3. $f(x) = \dfrac{3.7}{x}$ for $x = 26$ _____ $x = 0.92$ _____ $x = -14.1$ _____

EXPLORE

Two functions can be combined to form a composition of functions. For example, if $f(x) = 2x$ and $g(x) = x - 3$, we can find $f(g(x))$ for $x = 17$ by first finding $g(17) = 14$ and then substituting for $g(x)$ to find $f(14) = 28$.

EXAMPLE Let $f(x) = 3x^2 + 2$ and $g(x) = 6x - 3$. Find $g(f(3.2))$.

3 [×] 3.2 [x^2] [+] 2 [=] `32.72` [STO]   Finding $f(3.2)$ and storing it in memory

6 [×] [RCL] [−] 3 [=] `193.32`   Finding $g(f(3.2))$

$g(f(3.2)) = 193.32$

Let $f(x) = 32x$, $g(x) = -1.2x^2$, and $h(x) = 4.9x$. Find

4. $f(h(3))$ _____   **5.** $h(f(3))$ _____

6. $g(f(5.2))$ _____   **7.** $f(g(5.2))$ _____

8. $g(h(-13))$ _____   **9.** $h(g(-13))$ _____

10. Try some other numbers for each composition. Does:

$f(h(x)) = h(f(x))$? _____ $g(f(x)) = f(g(x))$? _____ $g(h(x)) = h(g(x))$? _____

Quadratic Functions

The x-coordinate of the vertex of the parabola $y = ax^2 + bx + c$ is $-\dfrac{b}{2a}$.

You can use a calculator to find the x-coordinate, substitute it in the original equation, and find the y-coordinate.

EXAMPLE   Find the coordinates of the vertex of $y = 14x^2 + 6.44x + 3.1$.
First solve for the x-coordinate and store it in the memory:
$b = 6.44$ and $a = 14$

6.44 $\boxed{\div}$ $\boxed{(}$ 2 $\boxed{\times}$ 14 $\boxed{)}$ $\boxed{=}$ $\mathsf{0.23}$ $\boxed{+/-}$ $\mathsf{-0.23}$ $\boxed{\text{STO}}$

Now solve for $y = 14x^2 + 6.44x + 31$.

14 $\boxed{\times}$ $\boxed{\text{RCL}}$ $\boxed{x^2}$ $\boxed{+}$ 6.44 $\boxed{\times}$ $\boxed{\text{RCL}}$ $\boxed{+}$ 3.1 $\boxed{=}$ $\mathsf{2.3594}$

The coordinates of the vertex are $(-0.23, 2.3594)$.

PRACTICE

Find the coordinates of the vertex of each parabola. Round to the nearest thousandth.

1. $y = 2x^2 + 12x - 3$ _____

2. $y = 5x^2 - 8x + 6$ _____

3. $y = -71x^2 - 5x + 19$ _____

4. $y = \dfrac{8}{3}x^2 - 1.6x - 5.1$ _____

5. $y = -9.9x^2 + 19.8x + 9.7$ _____

6. $y = 1.5x^2 + 32.74x - 0.8$ _____

EXPLORE

7. A parabola crosses the x-axis at 2 points. What is the value of y at each of those points? _____

8. Solve the equation $x^2 - 5.29 = 0$ to determine where the parabola $y = x^2 - 5.29$ crosses the x-axis. $x =$ _____

9. What happens when you try to solve the equation $x^2 + 12.88 = 0$ in an effort to determine where the parabola $y = x^2 + 12.88$ crosses the x-axis? _____

10. Where does the parabola $y = x^2 + 12.88$ cross the x-axis? _____

11. How many solutions does $x^2 - 64 = 0$ have? _____

How many times does the parabola $y = x^2 - 64$ cross the x-axis? _____

12. How many solutions does $x^2 + 169 = 0$ have? _____
How many times does the parabola $y = x^2 + 169$ cross the x-axis? _____

Direct Variation

Equations of direct variation have the form $y = kx$. The equation is perfectly constructed for use with the calculator's constant function.

EXAMPLE An equation of variation is $y = 3.5x$. Find y when $x = 4$, $x = 6$, and $x = -0.6$.
Program the calculator to multiply by the given value of k:

3.5 $\boxed{\times}$ $\boxed{=}$ (If your calculator has a $\boxed{K}$ key, press it before $\boxed{=}$.)

Enter each value of x and press $\boxed{=}$:

4 $\boxed{=}$ 14 6 $\boxed{=}$ 21 0.6 $\boxed{+/-}$ $\boxed{=}$ -2.1

The desired values of y are 14, 21, and -2.1.

PRACTICE

Find y for the given values of x.

1. Equation of variation: $y = 9.4x$ $x = 6$ $y =$ _____

$x = -5.9$ $y =$ _____

EXPLORE

When the equation of variation is not known, it can be found from a known pair of values.

EXAMPLE One pair of values that satisfies an equation of direct variation is $x = 5$, $y = 24.5$. Find y when $x = 4$.

We substitute to find k: $y = kx$
$$24.5 = k(5)$$
$$k = \frac{24.5}{5} = 24.5 \boxed{\div} 5 \boxed{=} \; 4.9$$

The equation of variation is $y = 4.9x$.
When $x = 4$, $y = 4.9(4) = 19.6$.

Find the equation of variation. Then evaluate y for the given values of x.

2. Known pair of values: $x = 17$ Find y: $x = 4.6$ $y =$ _____
$y = 119$ $x = -13.5$ $y =$ _____

Linear functions

The function $T = 0.25n + 40$, where n is the number of times a cricket chirps per minute, gives a good approximation of the Farenheit temperature (T). Find the temperature at the following chirp frequencies.

3. 84 chirps per minute _____   **4.** 128 chirps per minute _____

5. 32 chirps per minute _____   **6.** 4 chirps per *second* _____

7. At what temperature do crickets stop chirping?   _____

The Quadratic Formula

When solving quadratic equations on a calculator, first evaluate the square root of the discriminant and store it in memory. Then calculate the two solutions of the equation.

EXAMPLE   Solve $3x^2 - 8x + 2 = 0$ using the quadratic formula.
By the quadratic formula,

$$x = \frac{-(-8) \pm \sqrt{(-8)^2 - 4(3)(2)}}{2(3)}$$

We evaluate the discriminant, take the square root, and store the result.

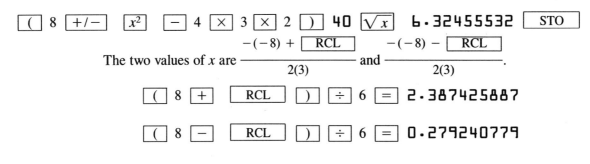

The two values of x are $\dfrac{-(-8) + \boxed{\text{RCL}}}{2(3)}$ and $\dfrac{-(-8) - \boxed{\text{RCL}}}{2(3)}$.

$\boxed{(}$ 8 $\boxed{+}$ $\boxed{\text{RCL}}$ $\boxed{)}$ $\boxed{\div}$ 6 $\boxed{=}$ 2.387425887

$\boxed{(}$ 8 $\boxed{-}$ $\boxed{\text{RCL}}$ $\boxed{)}$ $\boxed{\div}$ 6 $\boxed{=}$ 0.279240779

The solutions to the equation, rounded to the nearest hundredth,
are $x = 2.39$ and $x = 0.28$.

PRACTICE

Solve using the quadratic formula. Round to the nearest hundredth.

1. $x^2 + 4x - 6 = 0$ $x_1 = $ _____ $x_2 = $ _____

2. $-6x^2 - 9x + 7 = 0$ $x_1 = $ _____ $x_2 = $ _____

EXPLORE

Find the value of the discriminant (D) and determine the number of real-number solutions.

3. $5x^2 + 8x + 4.6 = 0$ $D = $ _____   Number of solutions = _____

4. $22.05x^2 - 21x + 5 = 0$ $D = $ _____   Number of solutions = _____

5. The discriminant of a certain quadratic equation is 228.
If $a = 8$ and $c = 3$, find the value of b.   _____

6. The discriminant of a certain quadratic equation is 1729.
If $a = -24$ and $c = -11.25$, find the value of b.   _____

The solution of a certain quadratic equation is $x = \dfrac{-11 \pm \sqrt{481}}{36}$.

7. Find the value of a. _____   **8.** Find the value of b. _____

9. Find the value of c. _____   **10.** What is the equation? _____

Finding Trigonometric Values

To find the sine, cosine, or tangent of a given angle, enter the angle, then press | SIN | , | COS | ,
or | TAN | .

EXAMPLE Find cos 28.3°.

28.3 | COS | 0.880477353

To the nearest thousandth, cos 28.3° = 0.880.

PRACTICE

Find these trigonometric values. Round to the nearest thousandth.

1. sin 45° _____

2. tan 28° _____

3. cos 150° _____

4. tan 0.42° _____

5. sin 90° _____

6. cos 37.243° _____

EXPLORE

7. The diagram shows three right triangles with successively larger
angle *A*'s. As angle *A* gets larger, would you expect its tangent to
get larger, smaller, or remain about the same?

_____

8. Test your answer to Exercise 7 by completing this table of values. Round to the nearest hundredth.

∠ A	tan A
80°	_____
89°	_____
89.9°	_____

∠ A	tan A
89.999°	_____
89.999999°	_____

9. Find tan 90°. Explain the answer given by your calculator.

_____

Degrees (°) are subdivided into minutes (′) and seconds (″).

1° = 60′   1′ = 60″   1° = 3600″

Many calculators will convert between decimal degrees and degrees, minutes, and seconds. To convert
from degrees, minutes, and seconds to decimal degrees, use the ►DD function (or DMS►DD).

EXAMPLE Find sin 22° 7′ 30″.

First convert the angle to a decimal degree, and then find the sine. If the number of minutes
or seconds has only 1 digit, insert a 0 before the single digit.

22.0730 | ►DD | 22.125 | SIN | 0.376628501

To the nearest thousandth, sin 22° 7′ 30″ = 0.377.

Find these trigonometric values. Round to the nearest thousandth.

10. cos 47°28′39″ _____

11. tan 82°16′47″ _____

12. sin 136°2′18″ _____

Finding Angles

If you know the sine, cosine, or tangent of an angle, you can find the angle itself using the SIN^{-1}, COS^{-1}, or TAN^{-1} functions. These functions are often accessed by using INV or 2nd with SIN, COS, and TAN respectively.

EXAMPLE   Find angle A if $\cos A = 0.8911$.

0.8911 $\boxed{COS^{-1}}$ **2Ь·98820052**

Angle A measures about 27°.

PRACTICE

Find angle A to the nearest degree.

1. $\sin A = 0.7313$ _____

2. $\tan A = 0.1051$ _____

3. $\cos A = 0.1564$ _____

4. $\tan A = 11.43$ _____

5. $\sin A = 0.7955$ _____

6. $\cos A = 0.9603$ _____

EXPLORE

Complete the table. Round to the nearest degree.

	$\sin A$	$\cos B$	$\angle A$	$\angle B$	$\angle A + \angle B$
7.	0.3746	0.3746			
8.	0.6428	0.6428			
9.	0.0523	0.0523			
10.	0.8746	0.8746			

11. Use the results you obtained above to complete the following statement: If the sine of one angle equals the cosine of another angle, the sum of the angles is _____

Complete the table. Round to the nearest ten-thousandth.

A	24°	39°	50°
12. $\sin A$			
13. $\cos A$			
14. $\dfrac{\sin A}{\cos A}$			
15. $\tan A$			

16. Use the results you obtained above to complete the following statement: If the sine of an angle is divided by the cosine of the same angle, the quotient is _____

Solving Right Triangles

If you know the measure of an angle and the length of a side of a right triangle, you can find the lengths of the other sides.

EXAMPLE In right triangle ABC, $B = 72°$ and $a = 14$ in. Find b.

The ratio relating a, b, and $\angle B$ is the tangent.

$$\tan B = \frac{b}{a}$$

$$\tan 72° = \frac{b}{14}$$

$$14(\tan 72°) = b$$

14 $\boxed{\times}$ 72 $\boxed{\text{TAN}}$ $\boxed{=}$ 43.08756952

Side b is about 43.1 in. in length.

PRACTICE

Find the required length. Round to the nearest tenth.

1. $c = 40$ m, $42°$

Find a. _____

2. $53.25°$, $b = 3.9$ km

Find a. _____

3. $14.36°$, $a = 2173$ mm

Find c. _____

EXPLORE

Find $\angle B$. Round to the nearest tenth.

4. $b = 387$ mm, $a = 516$ mm

$\angle B =$ _____

5. $b = 129.4$ m, $c = 177.6$ m

$\angle B =$ _____

6. $38.9°$

$\angle B =$ _____

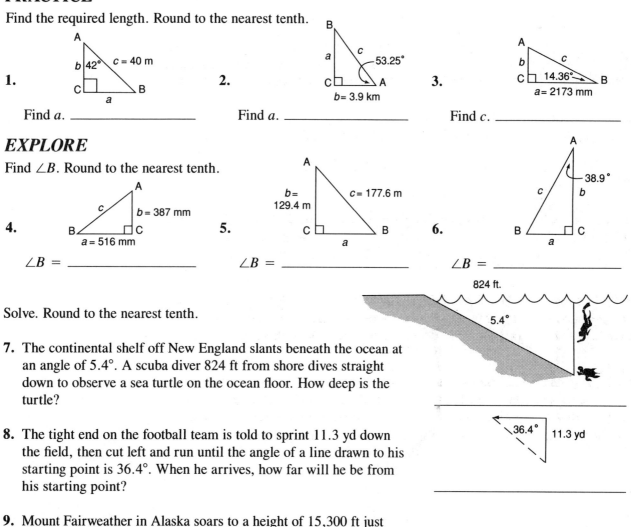

Solve. Round to the nearest tenth.

7. The continental shelf off New England slants beneath the ocean at an angle of 5.4°. A scuba diver 824 ft from shore dives straight down to observe a sea turtle on the ocean floor. How deep is the turtle?

8. The tight end on the football team is told to sprint 11.3 yd down the field, then cut left and run until the angle of a line drawn to his starting point is 36.4°. When he arrives, how far will he be from his starting point?

_____

9. Mount Fairweather in Alaska soars to a height of 15,300 ft just 14.3 miles from the Pacific coast. What is the angle of elevation of the summit of the mountain as observed from the coast? (1 mi = 5280 ft)

_____

Measures of Central Tendency

The $\Sigma+$ and $\bar{x}$ functions on your calculator allow you to analyze statistical data easily. In order to use these functions, you may have to press ⎡MODE⎤ ⎡STAT⎤ to put your calculator in statistics mode. (Some calculators will automatically go into statistics mode when the ⎡$\Sigma+$⎤ key is pressed.)

EXAMPLE   Find the mean of this set of temperature readings:

81.3° F, 107.6° F, 72.8° F, 93.5° F, and 101.8° F

Make sure the calculator is in statistics mode, then enter each temperature, followed by $\Sigma+$.

81.3 ⎡$\Sigma+$⎤   107.6 ⎡$\Sigma+$⎤   72.8 ⎡$\Sigma+$⎤   93.5 ⎡$\Sigma+$⎤   101.8 ⎡$\Sigma+$⎤

Notice that each time you press ⎡$\Sigma+$⎤ , the calculator tells you how many numbers you have entered.

To find the mean, press ⎡$\bar{x}$⎤ : **9l.4**

The mean temperature is 91.4° F.

After finding a mean, clear your calculator for the next calculation by pressing ⎡AC/ON⎤ .

PRACTICE

1. Find the mean of these tree heights. Round to the nearest hundredth.
   289 ft, 307 ft, 362 ft, 247 ft, 268 ft, 291 ft, 344 ft, 307 ft
   If you make a mistake you can remove a number by using the
   $\Sigma-$ function.   _____

2. Without clearing your calculator, press 247 ⎡$\Sigma-$⎤ 268
   ⎡$\Sigma-$⎤ ⎡$\bar{x}$⎤ to find the mean of the 6 greatest heights.   _____

EXPLORE

3. After pressing ⎡$\Sigma+$⎤ for the last time when entering a set of
   data to find the mean, Todd saw that the display on his calculator
   read 37. If he arranges his values in order, which value will be the
   median?   _____

Solve. Round to the nearest hundredth.

4. Find the mean of the first 10 perfect squares. (Enter 1 ⎡x^2⎤
   ⎡$\Sigma+$⎤ 2 ⎡x^2⎤ ⎡$\Sigma+$⎤ etc.)   _____

5. Find the mean of sin 10°, sin 20°, sin 30°, sin 40°, sin 50°, sin 60°,
   sin 70°, sin 80°, and sin 90°.   _____

6. Find the mean of $\frac{1}{1}, \frac{1}{2}, \frac{1}{3}, \frac{1}{4}, \frac{1}{5}, \frac{1}{6}, \frac{1}{7}, \frac{1}{8}, \frac{1}{9}$, and $\frac{1}{10}$. (Use the reciprocal
   key ⎡$1/x$⎤ and the statistics keys.)   _____

7. Find the mean of $\sqrt{10}, \sqrt[3]{10}, \sqrt[4]{10},$ and $\sqrt[5]{10}$.   _____

Spreadsheet Activities

The Spreadsheet Activities provide the opportunity for students to use spreadsheets as a tool for solving problems. Each activity presents a model spreadsheet with detailed instructions on how to enter all the data, labels, and formulas. Exercises require students to use the model, make modifications, and sometimes create new models.

The models presented are designed to work with the Appleworks spreadsheet software. Other spreadsheet software can be used, however, often without change. In all cases, students will need an introduction to spreadsheets and the specific program being used. Formatting commands have not been included so computer screens may not match the DISPLAY with respect to alignment or number of decimal places.

Listed below are some specific conventions being used in these spreadsheet models:

1. In each example the screen display is shown first, followed by the formulas. Longer formulas are given below the formulas representation.

2. Calculation on a spreadsheet is done either row-by-row or column-by-column, and this order must be set. The order of calculation for the spreadsheet models given is indicated by

   Order: Row   or   Order: Column

3. Duplicate formulas are often copied down a column or across a row to expedite preparation of the spreadsheet model. When a formula is copied, the spreadsheet program will need to be told whether the variables are to be copied with *no change* or *relative* to the row or column in which it is being placed. To indicate that a formula, say $+B1*A3*B3$, is to be copied from cell C3 down column C into cells C4 through C10, with the value in B1 to be the same in every formula (*no change*), but the values in A3 and B3 to change to A4 and B4 in cell C4, to A5 and B5 in cell C5, etc., we write

   Copy Down B3: *NRR*

Spreadsheets have built-in functions, features to improve the display, and many other helpful commands. You should consult your manual for details of these features and the conventions of the spreadsheet. Two such conventions are emphasized here.

1. An expression that starts with a number or operation sign is treated as a value. An expression that starts with a letter is treated as a label. If a formula begins with the letter of a cell address, prefix it with a $+$ sign to ensure that it will be treated as a formula (e.g., $+A3+B2$). An expression that starts with a double quote is treated as a label (e.g., "6 years).

2. Some spreadsheets, including AppleWorks®, perform operations in a strict left-to-right order. Thus, the value of $2*4+3*7$ will be 77. To produce 29, use $(2*4)+(3*7)$.

Additional commands and functions are given in the activities as they are needed. You should consult your spreadsheet manual for detailed instructions pertaining to all relevant features of the spreadsheet program.

Using Formulas

A spreadsheet can be programmed with formulas, which can do many calculations very quickly. New data can be entered and the new answers calculated in a few seconds.

EXAMPLE
Design a spreadsheet model to compute baseball batting and slugging averages where,

AB = At Bats (the number of times at bat)
1B = Singles (the number of one-base hits)
2B = Doubles (the number of two-base hits)
3B = Triples (the number of three-base hits)
HR = Home Runs (the number of four-base hits)
Avg. = Batting average (Total hits/At Bats)
Slug. = Slugging average (Total bases/At Bats)

When completed, the spreadsheet display will look like this. Steps for creating this model are listed on the next page.

Display

	A	B	C	D	E	F	G	H
1	NAME	AB	1B	2B	3B	HR	AVG.	SLUG.
2	RAMOS	100	33	10	2	1	.460	.630
3	YOUNG	250	7	10	10	30	.228	.708
4	WONG	200	46	0	0	0	.230	.230
⋮	⋮	⋮	⋮	⋮	⋮	⋮		
18	TEAM	2329	535	87	24	72	.308	.459

Formulas

	A	B	C	D	E	F	G	H
1	NAME	``AB	``1B	``2B	``3B	``HR	``AVG.	``SLUG.
2	RAMOS	100	33	10	2	1	[G2]	[H2]
3	YOUNG	250	7	10	10	30	[G3]	[H3]
4	WONG	200	46	0	0	0	[G4]	[H4]
⋮	⋮	⋮	⋮	⋮	⋮	⋮		
18	TEAM	@SUM (B2,, B17)	@SUM (C2,, C17)	@SUM (D2,, D17)	@SUM (E2,, E17)	@SUM (F2,, F17)	[G18]	[H18]

G2: (C2+D2+E2+F2)/B2
G3: (C3+D3+E3+F3)/B3
G18: (C18+D18+E18+F18)/B18

H2: (C2+(2*D2)+(3*E2)+(4*F2))/B2
H3: (C3+(2*D3)+(3*E3)+(4*F3))/B3
H18: (C18+(2*D18)+(3*E18)+ (4*F18))/B18

Copy B18 Across: *RR*; G2, H2 Down: *RRRRR*   Order: Row

*You will copy the formula in cell B18 across, with both variables copied *relatively*. You will copy the formulas in cells G2 and H2 down, with all variables copied *relatively*.

Steps for creating the model:

1. Enter the labels in row 1 as shown above. Enter the players' names in column A. (Note that more players can be added in rows 5 through 17.) Enter the statistics for each player in column B through column F. Enter the word TEAM in cell A18.
2. Enter the formula for Ramos' batting average, (C2 + D2 + E2 + F2)/B2 in cell G2.
3. Enter the formula for Ramos' slugging average, (C2 + (2*D2) + (3*E2) + (4*F2))/B2 in cell H2.
4. Copy the formulas in cells G2 and H2 down the column for the other players in rows 3 to 18 using the COPY command. All variables are copied *relatively* as the values of these variables change for each player.
5. Enter the formulas for the team totals in row 18. Enter the total At Bats by entering @SUM(B2 . . B17) in cell B18. This calculates the sum of the values in cells B2 through B17. Copy this formula to cells C18 through F18 with both variables *relative*.

Note that the TEAM totals shown on the display are for more players than the four shown. This model allows 17 players. For more than 17 players, use the INSERT command to insert more rows between rows 17 and 18. Then copy the formulas in row 17 down the column.

EXERCISES

1. Use the spreadsheet model to play "what if," by entering different statistics for the players and/or adding other players to the team. Then determine if it is possible for a player to have a higher batting average, but a lower slugging average than another player. Explain your answer.

2. Find the number of ways in which a batter with 20 At Bats can have a 0.400 batting average and a 0.600 slugging average.

3. A pitcher's ERA (Earned Run Average) is $9e/i$, where e = earned runs, and i = innings pitched. Construct a spreadsheet model that will compute individual and team ERAs.

4. Design a spreadsheet model that computes batting averages when batting against right-handed pitchers and left-handed pitchers as well as the overall batting average. Using the statistics below, what surprising result do you observe?

Name	Left-Handed			Right-Handed			Overall		
	AB	H	Avg.	AB	H	Avg.	AB	H	Avg.
Garcia	300	70	_____	90	34	_____	_____	_____	_____
Lutz	70	13	_____	140	46	_____	_____	_____	_____

Decimal Expansions

Recall that a rational number can be expressed as either a terminating decimal or a repeating decimal. Computers and calculators are programmed to represent decimals to a limited number of digits. We can create a spreadsheet model that will find as many digits as we want.

A fraction, such as 3/22, can be converted to a decimal by dividing the denominator of the fraction (22) into the numerator of the fraction (3). This decimal expansion is found using long division. We can express long division as a series of repeated divisions.

$$\begin{array}{r} .13636\ldots \\ 22\overline{)3.00000} \\ 2\,2 \\ \hline 80 \\ 66 \\ \hline 66 \\ \hline 4 \end{array}$$
or
$$\begin{array}{r} 1 \\ 22\overline{)30} \\ 22 \\ \hline 8 \end{array} \quad \begin{array}{r} 3 \\ 22\overline{)80} \\ 66 \\ \hline 14 \end{array} \quad \begin{array}{r} 6 \\ 22\overline{)140} \\ 132 \\ \hline 8 \end{array} \quad \begin{array}{r} 3 \\ 22\overline{)80} \\ 66 \\ \hline 14 \end{array}$$

Notice that the previous remainder times ten is divided by the denominator (22) of the fraction. This yields an integer quotient (the next digit) and a new remainder.

EXAMPLE   Design a spreadsheet that will find the decimal expansion for a fraction.

Display

	A	B
1	NUM	DEN
2	3	22
3	REM	QUO
4	3	1
5	8	3
6	14	6
7	8	3
8	14	6

$\dfrac{3}{22} = .13636$ to five decimal places

Formulas

	A	B
1	NUMERATOR	DENOMINATOR
2	3	22
3	REMAINDER	QUOTIENT
4	+A2	@INT(10*A4/B2)
5	(10*A4)-(B2*B4)	@INT(10*A5/B2)
6	(10*A5)-(B2*B5)	@INT(10*A6/B2)
7	(10*A6)-(B2*B6)	@INT(10*A7/B2)
8	(10*A7)-(B2*B7)	@INT(10*A8/B2)

Order: Row
Copy A5 Down: *RNR*;
Copy B4 Down: *RN*

Steps for creating the model:

1. Enter the labels shown in cells A1, B1, A3, and B3. Enter the numerator (3) and denominator (22) in cells A2 and B2 respectively.
2. Enter the formula +A2 in cell A4, which places the numerator (3) in position for the first division.
3. Enter @INT(10*A4/B2) in cell B4. This is the first division. The INT function is used so that we will get only the integer portion of the division.
4. The remainder from this division is computed in cell A5. Enter (10*A4) − (B2*B4) in A5.
5. Copy the formulas in cells B4 and A5 down their columns for the repeated computations of divisions and remainders. Cell A5 is copied down the column with the variables A4, B2, and B4 copied *relatively*, with *no change*, and *relatively* respectively. Cell B4 is copied down the column with the variables A4 copied *relatively* and B2 with *no change*.

Note that this spreadsheet must be calculated row-by-row.

EXERCISES

1. Find decimal expansions for the following fractions. Note which fractions terminate and which repeat. Look for a pattern to determine which fractions have terminating decimal expansions.

   a. $\frac{1}{2}$ **b.** $\frac{3}{8}$ **c.** $\frac{5}{7}$ **d.** $\frac{13}{60}$ **e.** $\frac{3}{500}$ **f.** $\frac{317}{500}$

2. The decimal expansions of each of the following fractions terminate, but have various lengths. Find decimal expansions for these fractions. Can you discover a pattern for the length of the decimal expansion?

   a. $\frac{1}{2}$ **b.** $\frac{3}{8}$ **c.** $\frac{3}{500}$ **d.** $\frac{7}{20}$ **e.** $\frac{19}{50}$ **f.** $\frac{23}{2000}$ **g.** $\frac{47}{64}$

3. The decimal expansions of each of the following fractions eventually repeat. Find decimal expansions for these fractions. Find enough digits to determine the repeated digits. Look for patterns.

   a. $\frac{1}{3}$ **b.** $\frac{1}{7}$ **c.** $\frac{1}{300}$ **d.** $\frac{7}{11}$ **e.** $\frac{7}{22}$ **f.** $\frac{8}{35}$ **g.** $\frac{8}{140}$

4. The Fibonacci numbers 1, 1, 2, 3, 5, 8, 13, . . . are generated by defining the first two to be 1, and then forming others as the sums of the two previous ones. Use a spreadsheet to generate these numbers. Also form quotients of successive terms in the sequence. What do you observe about these ratios?

Polynomial Multiplication

Although algebraic operations involving both constants and variables cannot be directly represented on a spreadsheet, they can frequently be performed by operating only with the coefficients of the variables.

Recall how polynomials are multiplied.

Multiply $(5 + 4x - 2x^2)(2 + 3x + 4x^2)$

$$
\begin{array}{r}
5 + 4x - 2x^2 \\
2 + 3x + 4x^2 \\
\hline
10 + 8x - 4x^2 \\
15x + 12x^2 - 6x^3 \\
20x^2 + 16x^3 - 8x^4 \\
\hline
10 + 23x + 28x^2 + 10x^3 - 8x^4
\end{array}
$$

EXAMPLE   Design a spreadsheet model to perform the above polynomial multiplication.

Display

	A	B	C	D	E	F
1	X^0	X^1	X^2	X^3	X^4	X^5
2	5	4	-2			
3	2	3	4			
4						
5	10	8	-4	0	0	0
6		15	12	-6	0	0
7			20	16	-8	0
8						
9	10	23	28	10	-8	0

The polynomials and products are represented by their coefficients of ascending powers of x.

Order: Row
Copy A5, B6, C7 Across: *NR*
Copy A9 Across: *RR*

Formulas

	A	B	C	D	E	F
1	` ` X^0	` ` X^1	` ` X^2	` ` X^3	` ` X^4	` ` X^5
2	5	4	-2			
3	2	3	4			
4	` ` _____	` ` _____	` ` _____	` ` _____	` ` _____	` ` _____
5	+A3*A2	+A3*B2	+A3*C2	+A3*D2		
6		+B3*A2	+B3*B2	+B3*C2	+B3*D2	
7			+C3*A2	+C3*B2	+C3*C2	+C3*D2
8	` ` _____	` ` _____	` ` _____	` ` _____	` ` _____	` ` _____
9	@SUM (A5,,A7)	@SUM (B5,,B7)	@SUM (C5,,C7)	@SUM (D5,,D7)	@SUM (E5,,E7)	@SUM (F5,,F7)

Steps for creating the model:

1. Enter the labels in rows 1, 4, and 8 as shown. Notice that a carat (ˆ) is used to show that the next number is an exponent.
2. Enter the coefficients of the polynomial $5 + 4x - 2x^2$ in cells A2, B2, and C2. Enter the coefficients of $2 + 3x + 4x^2$ in A3, B3, and C3. Note the order of the terms.
3. Enter the formulas in rows 5, 6, and 7 as shown to multiply each coefficient of one polynomial by each coefficient of the other polynomial.
4. Each column can be added by using addition formulas or by using the SUM function. The formula @SUM(A5. .A7) is the same as $+A5 + A6 + A7$. Enter these sum formulas in row 9 as shown.

This model permits a product of degree 5. To allow higher degrees for the product, copy the formulas in row 5 through 9 into columns on the right.

EXERCISES

1. Multiply the following polynomials.
   a. $(-7 + 5x + 3x^2)(6 + x + 4x^2 + 5x^3)$ b. $(1 - 2x + x^2)(8 + x^3 + 5x^4)$

2. Square the following polynomials. Look for a pattern.
   a. $(1 + 4x + 4x^2)^2$ b. $(3 + x + x^2)^2$ c. $(1 + x + 2x^2)^2$

3. Modify the spreadsheet model so that the lower polynomial can be of degree greater than 2. Use the INSERT command to insert additional rows between rows 7 and 8. Enter formulas into these rows as before, and modify the bottom row. Then multiply the following polynomials.
   a. $(-1 + x)(1 + x + x^2 + x^3)$ b. $(1 + 7x + x^2 + 4x^4)(1 + x^2 + 3x^3)$

4. Design a model for polynomial addition. Use the model to add polynomials in Lesson 5-7.

5. Design a model for polynomial subtraction. Use the model to subtract polynomials in Lesson 5-8.

For use with Lesson 7-7

Lines

If we have data that is linearly related, we can determine a linear function from the data and predict other data using the function.

Recall that the equation of a line is $y = mx + b$, where:

(x, y) is any point on the line

m is the slope of the line

b is the y-intercept

EXAMPLE

Design a spreadsheet that will determine the equation of a line that contains the points $(3, 2)$ and $(4, -2)$. Then determine other points on the line.

Display

	A	B	C	D
1	POINTS	X	Y	
2	(X1,Y1):	3	2	
3	(X2,Y2):	4	-2	
4				
5	SLOPE=	-4		
6	Y-INT=	14		
7	Y =	-4	X+	14
8				
9		X	Y	
10		5	-6	
11		-1	18	
12		2	6	
13		4	-2	

Formulas

	A	B	C	D
1	POINTS	X	Y	
2	``(X1,Y1):	3	2	
3	``(X2,Y2):	4	-2	
4				
5	SLOPE=	[B5]		
6	Y-INT=	-B5*B2+C2		
7	Y=	+B5	``X+	+B6
8				
9		``X	``Y	
10		5	+B5*B10+B6	
11		-1	+B5*B11+B6	
12		2	+B5*B12+B6	
13		4	+B5*B13+B6	
14		0	+B5*B14+B6	

Order: Column
Copy C10 Down: *NRN*

B5: (C3 - C2)/(B3 - B2)

Steps for creating the model:

1. Enter labels in rows 1 and 9, column A, and cell C7 as shown.
2. Enter the coordinates of the given points (3, 2), and (4, −2) in cells B2, C2, B3, and C3 as shown.
3. Enter the formulas for slope and y-intercept in cells B5 and B6 as shown.
4. In row 7, a combination of labels and formulas show the equation of the line. Enter +B5 and +B6, the cells where the slope and the y-intercept are computed, in cells B7 and D7 respectively.
5. Enter the formula shown in cell C10 to calculate y as $mx + b$ for the x value in cell B10. Copy the formula in C10 down the column. To find additional points on the line, enter more x values in column B.

EXERCISES

1. Use the spreadsheet model to convert temperatures from Fahrenheit to Celsius. Use two easily remembered points, water freezes at 32°F = 0°C and water boils at 212°F = 100° C. Find the Celsius value of 98.6°F. At what value is the temperature the same for both Fahrenheit and Celsius?

2. Scores on test A are linearly related to scores on test B. Two students' scores are A = 500, B = 100 and A = 680, B = 127. Find a linear equation relating A and B. Predict the score on a B test for a student whose A score is 700.

3. The value of a property is depreciated linearly. Its value ten years ago was $50,000, and its value today is $24,000.
   a. Determine an equation relating the property value to years.
   b. Find the property value 5 years from today.
   c. When will the property value be 0?
   d. Suppose the property is 15 years old today. Find the value of the property when it was new.

4. Parallel lines have the same slope. The slope of a line perpendicular to a line having slope m is $-1/m$. Using these results, the following extension of the model finds equations of lines that pass through a given point, and are parallel or perpendicular to a given line.

	F	G	H	I
1 . . .	POINT:	2	3	
2 . . .	PAR: Y =	+B5	``X+	-G2*G1+H1
3 . . .	PER: Y =	-1/B5	``X+	-G3*G1+H1

Find equations of the lines parallel and perpendicular to the line determined by (2, 2) and (4, −2) and passing through the point
a. (4, 7)   b. (−2, 5)   c. (3, −4)

Linear Applications

The profit (or loss) from a business is found by computing the income and subtracting the expenses. When the profit is zero, we say that the business breaks even. With a spreadsheet model, we can play "what-if" to quickly determine the effect on the profit of changing values such as the price or the number of units sold.

EXAMPLE

A class raises money selling t-shirts. The class must invest $300 in design materials and pay $2 for each t-shirt. They sell the t-shirts for $5 each. Design a spreadsheet to determine the income, expense, and profit for the sale of x units of shirts for various x.

Let x = number of t-shirts sold.
Then

Expense $= 2x + 300$	The expense of the t-shirts plus the fixed expense
Income $= 5x$	The price of the t-shirts times the number sold
Profit $= 5x - (2x + 300)$	Income $-$ Expense

Display

	A	B	C	D
1		EXP	INC	
2	UNIT	2	5	
3	FIXED	300		
4				
5	BREAKEV	X =	100	
6	50	=STEP		
7	UNITS	EXP	INC	PROF
8	0	300	0	-300
9	50	400	250	-150
10	100	500	500	0
11	150	600	750	150

Formulas

	A	B	C	D
1		EXPENSE	INCOME	
2	UNIT	2	5	
3	FIXED	300		
4				
5	BREAKEVEN	X =	(C3-B3)/(B2-C2)	
6	50	``=STEP		
7	UNITS	EXPENSE	INCOME	PROFIT
8	0	+B2*A8+B3	+C2*A8+C3	+C8-B8
9	+A8+A6	+B2*A9+B3	+C2*A9+C3	+C9-B9
10	+A9+A6	+B2*A10+B3	+C2*A10+C3	+C10-B10
11	+A10+A6	+B2*A11+B3	+C2*A11+C3	+C11-B11

Order: Row
Copy A9 Down: *RN*
Copy B8, C8 Down: *NRN*
Copy D8 Down: *RR*

Steps for creating the model:

1. Enter all labels as shown.
2. Enter the unit and fixed expenses in cells B2 and B3, and enter the unit income in cell C2.
3. Enter 0 in cell A8. Enter $+A8 + A6$ in cell A9, and copy this formula down as far as you wish. Note that this formula increases the number of units sold by the value in cell A6 for each row. By changing the value in cell A6, you can change the size of "steps" between x values examined.
4. Enter the formulas for expense, income, and profit in cells B8, C8, and D8 respectively as shown above. Copy these formulas down the column (to match column A), with *no change* for the expense and income references (columns B and C), but *relative* for column A references.

EXERCISES

1. Use the spreadsheet model to determine the number of t-shirts that must be sold in order to break even, and the number of t-shirts that must be sold in order to have a profit of $600.

2. What if the selling price is changed to $4, $3, or $6. What is the break-even number of t-shirts for each new selling price?

3. What if the cost per t-shirt is changed to $3, $4, or $1. What is the break-even number of t-shirts for each cost change?

4. Note that the break-even value occurs when the profit is zero. This occurs when the expense and the income are equal. This means that $2x + 300 = 5x$, where 2 is the value in cell B2, 300 in cell B3, and 5 in cell C2. Derive a formula for the value of x for the break-even point and put this in the spreadsheet on row 5.

5. How does the break-even value of x (number of t-shirts sold) change if the fixed cost is increased by $100? by $200? by $300?

6. A clothing firm is planning a new line of jackets. For the first year, the fixed cost for setting up the production line is $10,000. The cost to produce each jacket is $20. Each jacket will be sold for $100.
   a. Determine the number of jackets that will need to be sold to break even.
   b. Determine the number of jackets that will need to be sold to make a profit of $150,000.

7. Alpha Corporation rents cars for $24 per day plus 20¢ per mile. Beta Corporation rents cars for $20 per day plus 30¢ per mile. (Hint: Change the Expense column in the model to Alpha and change the Income column in the model to Beta. The Profit column now compares the cost of renting a car from each company.)
   a. For what daily mileage are the costs the same?
   b. Which offers a better rate for 100 miles?
   c. For what number of miles is Alpha's rate better?

8. Computer Info Inc. charges $10 per month plus $7 per minute for computer access to its information. Data Access Corp. charges $20 per month plus $5 per minute.
   a. For what number of minutes per month are the charges the same?
   b. If you plan to access the computer for 10 hours per month, which company offers a better rate?

9. A medical firm can do its own billing for an annual fixed cost of $20,000 and $1.25 per bill, or hire an outside firm to do the billing for an annual fixed cost of $5,000 and $2.00 per bill.
   a. For what annual number of bills are the two equal?
   b. For what annual number of bills is it cheaper to hire the outside firm?
   c. What is the effect if the outside firm raises its price to $2.50 per bill?

Population Growth

The population of the United States in 1988, 244 million people, is projected to grow at a rate of 0.7%, compounded annually. We can use a spreadsheet to display this yearly growth.

Let p_0 = the current population in millions (244)

r = projected growth rate as a decimal (0.007)

Then rp_0 = the increase in population after one year

Let p_1 = the population after one year

Then $p_1 = p_0 + rp_0$

$= (1 + r)p_0 \quad (1 + 0.007)(244) = 245.7$ million

Similarly,

$p_2 = (1 + r)p_1$ after 2 years

$p_3 = (1 + r)p_2$ after 3 years, and so on

EXAMPLE

Design a spreadsheet model to compare the projected populations of the United States and Mexico. For the United States use the initial population and annual growth rate above; for Mexico, use 82 million and 2.5%.

Display

	A	B	C
1		USA	MEXICO
2	RATE=	.007	.025
3	POP=	244	82
4	YEAR	USA	MEXICO
5	0	244.0	82.0
6	1	245.7	84.0
7	2	247.4	86.2
8	3	249.2	88.3

Formulas

	A	B	C
1		USA	MEXICO
2	RATE=	.007	.025
3	POP=	244	82
4	YEAR	USA	MEXICO
5	0	+B3	+C3
6	1+A5	(1+B2)*B5	(1+C2)*C5
7	1+A6	(1+B2)*B6	(1+C2)*C6
8	1+A7	(1+B2)*B7	(1+C2)*C7

Order: Row
Copy A6 Down: *R*
Copy B6, C6 Down: *NR*

Steps for creating the model:

1. Enter the labels in rows 1 and 4 and column A as shown.
2. Enter the national growth rates in cells B2 and C2 and the initial populations into cells B3 and C3.
3. In row 5 enter the initial year number, zero, and formulas for the initial populations, +B3 and +C3, as shown.
4. Enter the formula 1 + A5 into A6, and copy it down *relatively*. This generates consecutive numbers.

5. Enter the formulas shown for the population after one year in cells B6 and C6.
6. To reflect the formulas for the population after 2 years, 3 years, and so on, copy the formulas in B6 and C6 down the column. The growth rate references, B2 and C2, are copied with *no change* while the previous year's populations, B5 and C5, are copied *relatively*.

EXERCISES

1. Use the COPY command to extend the table for 100 years. Suppose that each country's growth continues at its present rate. When will Mexico's population reach that of the United States?
   What if Mexico's growth rate is only 2%—when will Mexico's population be the same as that of the United States?

2. Complete the chart below. Since the data given is for the year 1988, 1988 is year 0, 1989 is year 1, 1990 is year 2 and so on.

	India	China	Indonesia	Kenya
Population in 1988 (millions)	800	1,275	175	22.4
Growth Rate (in %)	2.1	1.3	2.1	3.9
Years to double	_____	_____	_____	_____
Population in 2020	_____	_____	_____	_____

3. Investigate the time it takes for a country's population to double at various rates. Then look for a pattern.

Growth rate	1%	2%	3%	4%	5%	6%	7%	8%	9%	10%	11%	12%
Years to double	___	___	___	___	___	___	___	___	___	___	___	___

4. The model can be used to project the future cost of consumer goods. Suppose that the inflation rate continues at a constant rate of 5%. Determine the future cost of the items below.

Item	Current	5 years	10 years	20 years	50 years
Bread	_____	_____	_____	_____	_____
Magazine	_____	_____	_____	_____	_____
College	_____	_____	_____	_____	_____
Auto	_____	_____	_____	_____	_____
House	_____	_____	_____	_____	_____

Investigate the effect of changing the inflation rate. Determine the inflation rate and the cost of these goods in your area, and determine the future cost of these (and other) goods.

Word Problems

Spreadsheets can be useful for solving problems using algebraic equations as well as using other strategies such as *Guess, Check, Revise*.

EXAMPLE 1

Working alone, Al can complete a job in 15 days, Sam in 20 days, and Mary in 10 days. Design a spreadsheet model to determine how long it will take them to complete the job if they work together.

Let t = days needed to complete the job as a team

Then we know that $\frac{1}{t}$ of the job can be done in one day by the team. Al, Sam, and Mary can each do

$\frac{1}{15}, \frac{1}{20}$, and $\frac{1}{10}$ of the job in one day respectively. Therefore,

$$\frac{1}{t} = \frac{1}{15} + \frac{1}{20} + \frac{1}{10} \text{ and } t = \frac{1}{\text{sum}}$$

Display

	A	B	C
1		DAYS/JOB	JOB/DAY
2	AL	15	0.067
3	SAM	20	0.050
4	MARY	10	0.100
5			
6	ALL,	JOB/DAY =	0.217
7	ALL,	DAYS/JOB =	4.615

Formulas

	A	B	C
1		DAYS/JOB	JOB/DAY
2	AL	15	1/B2
3	SAM	20	1/B3
4	MARY	10	1/B4
5			
6	ALL,	JOB/DAY =	@SUM(C2..C4)
7	ALL,	DAYS/JOB =	1/C6

Steps for creating the model:

1. Enter all labels as shown.
2. Enter in cells B2..B4 the days needed for each person to do the job.
3. Enter the formula for the portion of the job Al can do in one day in cell C2, and copy this formula down relatively for Sam and Mary.
4. Enter the formula for the sum of C2, C3, and C4 in C6 as shown.
5. The reciprocal of this sum is the solution for t, the days needed to complete the job together. Enter the formula 1/C6 in cell C7 as shown.

Note that spreadsheet solutions are always decimals, which are rounded or truncated.

EXAMPLE 2

One train travels 20 mph faster than another. One train travels 180 miles in the same time that the other goes 240 miles. Use a spreadsheet to determine how fast each train is going and how long each travels.

Display

	A	B	C	D
1	EXTRA	SPEED =	20	
2		DISTANCE	RATE	TIME
3	SLOWER	180	10	18
4	FASTER	240	30	8

Formulas

	A	B	C	D
1	EXTRA	SPEED =	20	
2		DISTANCE	RATE	TIME
3	SLOWER	180	10	+B3/C3
4	FASTER	240	+C1+C3	+B4/C4

Steps for creating the model:

1. Enter all labels as shown. Enter the distances, 180 and 240, in cells B3 and B4.
2. Enter the difference in speed, 20, in cell C1.
3. Enter the formulas shown above in C4, D3, and D4 for the rate of the faster train, and the time for each train ($t = d/r$).
4. Enter guesses for the rate of the slower train in cell C3 until you find a rate that will make the time equal for both trains.

EXERCISES

1. Suppose you can enable one of the workers in Example 1 to work twice as fast as usual. Whom should you choose in order to speed the completion of the job the most?

2. A tank can be filled in 18 hours by pipe A or in 24 hours by pipe B. How long will it take both pipes to fill the tank?

3. A tank can be filled in 12 hours by pipe A or in 18 hours by pipe B. It can be emptied in 18 hours by pipe C. If all pipes are open, how long will it take for the tank to fill up?

4. In Example 2, the output comes from a guess of 10. Since the times are different (D3 and D4), this is incorrect. Use *Guess* and *Check* to determine the rate that will make the times equal.

5. One car travels 40 km/h faster than another. While one car travels 150 km, the other goes 350 km. Find the speeds of the cars.

Square Roots and Cube Roots

Square roots and cube roots can be approximated using a *guess* and *revise* method.

If s is the square root of N, then $ss = N$, and $s = N/s$. If s is not the square root, then the average of s and N/s is a better estimate.

$$\frac{s + N/s}{2}$$

This can be repeated as many times as necessary.

Similarly, if c is the cube root of N, then $ccc = N$, and $c = N/cc$. If c is not the cube root, then the average of c, c, and N/cc is a better estimate.

$$\frac{c + c + N/cc}{3} = \frac{2c + N/cc}{3} \text{ or } \frac{2c + N/c^2}{3}$$

We can design a spreadsheet model that can do this computation and the repetitions of this computation very quickly.

EXAMPLE

Design a spreadsheet model to estimate the square root and cube root of a number.

Display

	A	B
1	10	= N
2	ESTIMATE	ESTIMATE
3	3	2
4	SQUARE	CUBE
5	ROOT	ROOT
6	3.00000	2.00000
7	3.16667	2.16667
8	3.16228	2.15450
9	3.16228	2.15443
10	3.16228	2.15443

$$\sqrt{10} \approx 3.16228 \qquad \sqrt[3]{10} \approx 2.15443$$

You can see that the estimates converge to an accurate decimal approximation of the square and cube roots. The more accurate your initial estimate, the more quickly this convergence occurs.

Formulas

	A	B
1	10	= N
2	ESTIMATE	ESTIMATE
3	3	2
4	SQUARE	CUBE
5	ROOT	ROOT
6	+A3	+B3
7	(A6+(A1/A6))/2	(2*B6+(A1/(B6^2)))/3
8	(A7+(A1/A7))/2	(2*B7+(A1/(B7^2)))/3
9	(A8+(A1/A8))/2	(2*B8+(A1/(B8^2)))/3
10	(A9+(A1/A9))/2	(2*B9+(A1/(B9^2)))/3

Steps for creating the model:

1. Enter the labels shown in cell B1 and rows 2, 4, and 5.
2. Enter the number for which roots are to be found in cell A1.
3. Enter your initial estimate for the roots in row 3. (3 and 2 are the estimates in the example.)
4. The initial values are copied into cells A6 and B6 by formula references, $+A3$ and $+B3$ respectively.
5. Enter the formulas shown in cells A7 and B7, which represent the first averaging step for each root. Copy these formulas down their columns.

EXERCISES

1. Extend the formulas down the column for 20 rows. Observe the effect of using various initial estimates for $\sqrt{27}$. Try 4, 20, 100, 1000, -2, and -5.

2. What happens if you try to find the square root of a negative number? a cube root of a negative number?

3. Based on the schemes for finding square and cube roots, try to discover and implement similar ways to approximate fourth roots, fifth roots, and so on. (If you can create a general formula, you may have discovered special cases of Newton's Method studied in calculus.)
   a. Use your spreadsheet to find the fourth root of 81, 100, 200, and 300.
   b. Use your spreadsheet to find the fifth root of 7776, 9000, 1000, and 300.

4. Use a spreadsheet to compute values of $n! = n(n - 1)(n - 2)(n-3) \ldots 3(2)(1)$, for $n = 1, 2, 3, \ldots$ For example, $4! = 4 \cdot 3 \cdot 2 \cdot 1 = 24$. Note that $1! = 1$ and $n! = n(n - 1)!$

Triangles and the Pythagorean Theorem

The Pythagorean Theorem, with a spreadsheet programmed to do the computations, can be used to investigate triangles.

The distance formula is based on the Pythagorean Theorem (see the Distance Formula in your book). The distance between any two points (x_1, y_1) and (x_2, y_2) is given by

$$\sqrt{(x_1 - x_2)^2 + (y_1 - y_2)^2}$$

We can also use the Pythagorean Theorem to determine whether the triangle is a right triangle, an acute triangle, or an obtuse triangle. If C is the largest angle, then c is the longest side.

If $c^2 = a^2 + b^2$, then C is a right angle and $\triangle ABC$ is a right triangle.

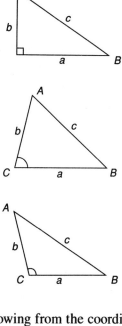

If $c^2 < a^2 + b^2$, then C is an acute angle and $\triangle ABC$ is an acute triangle.

If $c^2 > a^2 + b^2$, then C is an obtuse angle and $\triangle ABC$ is an obtuse triangle.

EXAMPLE

Design a spreadsheet model that will determine the following from the coordinates of the vertices of a triangle: the length of the sides of a triangle, the perimeter of this triangle, and whether the triangle is right, acute, or obtuse.

Display

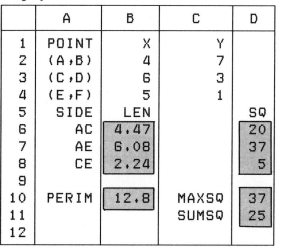

	A	B	C	D
1	POINT	X	Y	
2	(A,B)	4	7	
3	(C,D)	6	3	
4	(E,F)	5	1	
5	SIDE	LEN		SQ
6	AC	4.47		20
7	AE	6.08		37
8	CE	2.24		5
9				
10	PERIM	12.8	MAXSQ	37
11			SUMSQ	25
12				

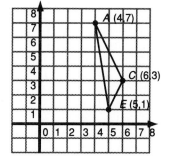

Formulas

	A	B	C	D
1	POINT	``X	``Y	
2	``(A,B)	4	7	
3	``(C,D)	6	3	
4	``(E,F)	5	1	
5	SIDE	LENGTH		SIDESQ
6	AC	[B6]		+B6*B6
7	AE	[B7]		+B7*B7
8	CE	[B8]		+B8*B8
9				
10	PERIM =	+B6+B7+B8	MAXSQ=	[D10]
11			SUMSQ=	[D11]
12				

Order: Column
Copy D6 Down: *RR*

```
B6: @SQRT((B3-B2)^2+((C3-C2)^2))
B7: @SQRT((B4-B2)^2+((C4-C2)^2))
B8: @SQRT((B4-B3)^2+((C4-C3)^2))
D10: @MAX(D6,.D8) D11: @SUM(D6,.D8)-D10
```

Steps for creating the model:

1. Enter labels as shown.
2. Enter the coordinates of the vertices in cells B2,C2; B3,C3; and B4,C4.
3. Enter the distance formula in cells B6, B7, and B8 as shown above. The SQRT function is used to compute the square root of the quantity in parentheses.
4. Enter the formula for perimeter in cell B10.
5. Enter the formula for the square of one side in cell D6, and copy it relatively to D7 and D8.
6. Enter the @MAX formula shown for cell D10. The MAX function outputs the maximum of all of the values listed in the parentheses. The formula finds the maximum of the squares of the sides.
7. Enter the formula shown for cell D11. This formula computes the sum of the squares of the two shorter sides of the triangle. (It does this by computing the sum of the squares of all three sides and subtracting the square of the largest side, the value in D10.)

Since the value in cell D10 is larger than the value in cell D11, the triangle is obtuse.

EXERCISES

1. Find the perimeter of each triangle. Determine whether the triangle is right, acute, or obtuse.
   a. (4, 7), (3, 5), (1, 8)   **b.** (4, 7), (3, 5), (1, 6)   **c.** (4, 7), (3, 5), (1, 4)

2. Create a spreadsheet model to compute the length of the following:
   a. the hypotenuse of a right triangle when the other two sides are known.
   b. the other side of a right triangle when one side and the hypotenuse are known.
   c. Use the model you created for Exercise 2a to find the length of the hypotenuse when the two sides are: 5 and 12; 31 and 480; 140 and 100.
   d. Use the model you created for Exercise 2b to find the third side when one side and the hypotenuse are 21 and 221; 13 and 20; 2 and 4.

3. If a right triangle has legs of length 3 and 4, then the hypotenuse of this triangle has length 5. (Check this using the spreadsheet model you created for Exercise 2a.) The integers 3, 4, and 5 are called a Pythagorean triple. Use the spreadsheet model that you created for Exercise 2 to find as many Pythagorean triples as you can. Can you find a pattern?

Quadratic Applications

A projectile is fired directly upward from a height of s_0 ft with an initial velocity of v_0 ft/sec. After t seconds its height will be $s = -16t^2 + v_0 t + s_0$, with velocity $v = -32t + v_0$. We can use a spreadsheet model to look at various aspects of the projectile's flight.

EXAMPLE

Design a spreadsheet model that will follow the height and velocity of a projectile every second as well as determine when the projectile is at ground level, what its velocity is when it lands, what the maximum height is, and when this height is attained for an initial height of 100 ft and initial velocity of 150 ft/sec.

Using the formulas for height (s) and velocity (v), we have

$$s = -16t^2 + 150t + 100 \quad \text{and} \quad v = -32t + 150$$

Display

	A	B	C
1	INITIAL	HT S=	100
2		VEL V =	150
3	TIME(0)	-.625	10,000
4	VEL(GR)		-170
5	TIME(M)		4.6875
6	HT(MAX)		451.56
7	T(SEC)	HT(FT)	VEL(F/S)
8	0	100	150
9	1	234	118
⋮	⋮	⋮	⋮
18	10	0	-170

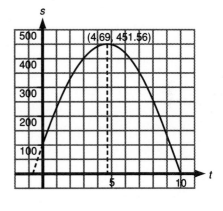

Formulas

	A	B	C
1	INITIAL	HT S=	100
2		VEL V =	150
3	TIME(0)	[B3]	[C3]
4	VEL(GR)		-32*C3+C2
5	TIME(M)		+C2/32
6	HT(MAX)		[C6]
7	T(SEC)	HT(FT)	VEL(F/S)
8	0	-16*A8*A8+(C2*A8)+C1	-32*A8+C2
9	1+A8	-16*A9*A9+(C2*A9)+C1	-32*A9+C2
⋮	⋮	⋮	⋮
18	1+A17	-16*A18*A18+(C2*A18)+C1	-32*A18+C2

Order: Row   Copy A9 Down: *R*; B8 Down: *RRNRN*; C8 Down: *RN*

```
B3: (C2-@SQRT((C2*C2)+(64*C1)))/32
C3: (C2+@SQRT((C2*C2)+(64*C1)))/32    C6: -16*C5*C5+(C2*C5)+C1
```

Steps for creating the model:

1. Enter labels as shown. Enter the initial height and initial velocity in cells C1 and C2.
2. The projectile will be at ground level when the height is zero, $s = 0$. Therefore, the solution to the equation $0 = -16t^2 + 150t + 100$ will give us the times when the projectile is at ground level. We use the quadratic equation, which are the formulas shown for cells B3 and C3, to solve this equation. (Note that $-4ac$ is $-4 \cdot -16 \cdot C1 = 64 \cdot C1$.)
3. The formula $v = -32t + 150$, where t is the time the projectile is at ground level, will give us the velocity of the projectile when it lands. Enter the formula $-32*C3+C2$ in cell C4.
4. The graph of the equation $s = -16t^2 + 150t + 100$ is a parabola. The vertex of this parabola is found using the formula $t = -\dfrac{b}{2a} = \dfrac{b}{-2(-16)}$. Enter $+C2/32$ in cell C5. Since this is the t value at the vertex, it is the time when the maximum height is attained.
5. The maximum height is the value of s at the vertex. This is found by evaluating the equation for the value found for t in cell C5. Enter $-16*C5*C5+(C2*C5)+C1$ in cell C6.
6. Enter 0 in cell A8, $1 + A8$ in cell A9, and copy this formula down the column.
7. Enter the formulas shown in cells B8 and C8 to determine the height and velocity for the time in cell A8. Copy cells B8 and C8 down the column.

EXERCISES

1. Use your output to sketch a graph of height as a function of time. What do you observe about the velocity as the projectile is going up? At its maximum elevation? As it is going down?

2. Leaving the initial velocity unchanged, investigate the effect of varying the initial height.

Initial height	0	100	200
Time of max. ht.	_____	_____	_____
Max. Height	_____	_____	_____
Time to ground	_____	_____	_____
Impact Velocity	_____	_____	_____

3. Set the initial height to 0 and investigate the effect of varying the initial velocity.

Initial velocity	0	75	150	300
Time of max. ht.	_____	_____	_____	_____
Max. Height	_____	_____	_____	_____
Time to ground	_____	_____	_____	_____
Impact Velocity	_____	_____	_____	_____

4. This model also works for objects that are dropped (C2 = 0) or thrown downward (C2 is negative). Suppose that a baseball is dropped from several buildings. How long does it take to hit the earth? How fast is it going when it hits?

Structure	Washington Monument	Empire State Building	Sears Tower	50' Pole
Height	555 ft	1250 ft	1454 ft	50 ft
Time	_____	_____	_____	_____
Impact Velocity	_____	_____	_____	_____

Trigonometry Applications

Spreadsheets can be used to solve problems involving trigonometric functions. Some spreadsheets have trigonometric functions such as @SIN and @TAN. These functions do not exist on all spreadsheets (e.g. AppleWorks). Alternative approaches are given for such spreadsheets.

Trigonometric functions in spreadsheets use radians as the unit of angle measure instead of degrees. We can convert from degrees to radians.

360 degrees $= 2\pi$ radians

If d and r are the degree and radian measures of an angle, then

$$\frac{r}{2\pi} = \frac{d}{360}$$

$$r = \frac{d(2\pi)}{360}$$

$$r = \frac{d\pi}{180}$$

EXAMPLE 1

Jane sees a fire from a tower that she thinks is 500 ft tall. She estimates that the angle of depression to the fire is 5°. What is the distance from the base of the tower to the fire? If the tower is actually 525 ft tall, and the angle of depression is 4°, by how much is the answer off?

Display

	A	B	C	D
1	HT	DEG	RADIANS	DIST
2	500	5	0.08727	5715.0
3	525	4	0.06981	7507.8

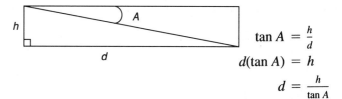

$$\tan A = \frac{h}{d}$$

$$d(\tan A) = h$$

$$d = \frac{h}{\tan A}$$

Formulas for spreadsheets with trigonometric functions

	A	B	C	D
1	HT	DEG	RADIANS	DIST
2	500	5	@PI*B2/180	+A2/@TAN(C2)
3	525	4	@PI*B3/180	+A3/@TAN(C3)

Order: Row
Copy C2, D2 Down: *RR*

For spreadsheets that do not have trigonometric functions, we can use an approximation of tan A.

$$\tan A = r + \frac{r^3}{3} + \frac{2r^5}{15}$$ where r is the radian equivalent of A

(This formula works best when A $<$ 30°. For larger angles, use the formula on the following page.)

Formulas for spreadsheets without trigonometric functions

	A	B	C	D	G
1	HT	DEG	RADIANS	DISTANCE	3.141593
2	500	5	+G1*B2/180	[D2]	
3	525	4	+G1*B3/180	[D3]	

Order: Row
Copy C2 Down: *NR*
Copy D2 Down: *RRRR*

```
D2: +A2/(C2+((C2^3)/3)+(2*(C2^5)/15))
D3: +A3/(C3+((C3^3)/3)+(2*(C3^5)/15))
```

Steps for creating the model:

1. Enter all labels. Enter heights in cells A2 and A3, and degree angle measures in B2 and B3.
2. Enter 3.141593 in cell G1 if necessary (if your spreadsheet does not recognize @PI).
3. Enter the formulas shown, using the formulas that work with your spreadsheet.
   (Note that small errors in the height and degree can produce a large error in the distance.)

If A is a positive angle less than or equal to 90° (≤80° for tan), we can compute the sine function correct to 4 digits by

$$\sin A = r - \frac{r^3}{6} + \frac{r^5}{120} - \frac{r^7}{5040} + \frac{r^9}{362880},$$ where r is the radian equivalent of A.

Then the other functions can be found in terms of $\sin A$.

$$\cos A = \sqrt{1 - s^2}, \text{ where } s = \sin A$$

$$\tan A = \frac{s}{\sqrt{1 - s^2}}, \text{ where } s = \sin A$$

EXERCISES

1. Enter $+D3 - D2$ in cell E3 to compute the error between the estimated height in cell D2 and the actual height in cell D3. Enter @ABS((D3 − D2)/D3) in cell F3 to compute the percent of error. Using Jane's estimates, what is the difference between her estimated distance to the fire and the actual distance? What is the percent of this error?

2. A pilot in a plane 3 km above the ground estimates that the angle of depression to a runway is 51°. What is the horizontal distance to the runway?

3. A line is attached to the top of a 100 m tower and stretched to the ground, where it makes an angle of 28° with the ground. How far from the base of the tower does the line contact the ground?

4. Maria and Ellen are directly across a river from an elm tree. Maria has heard that the elm tree is 500 feet from an oak tree that is downstream on the same side of the river as the elm tree. Maria estimates that when she faces the river at its edge, the line of sight to the oak tree makes an angle of 27° with the river as shown. Ellen estimates that the line of sight to the oak tree makes an angle of 24° with the river, and she thinks that the elm tree is 525 feet from the oak tree.
   a. Using Maria's estimations, approximately how wide is the river?
   b. Using Ellen's estimations, approximately how wide is the river?
   c. If the tree is actually 517 feet from the oak tree, and the angle is actually 29°, how wide is the river? Whose estimate is closer?

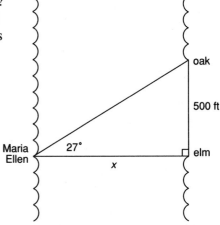

5. Paul is flying a kite with 200 feet of string out. If the angle of elevation is 60°, what is the height of the kite? (Hint, you will need to create a modified spreadsheet model first.)

Statistics

Most spreadsheets have a set of functions and commands designed specifically for statistical applications. Calculations, such as finding the mean, depend not only on the values of the data, but also depend on the number of pieces of data. The spreadsheet function @COUNT does such a count.

EXAMPLE 1

Design a spreadsheet model to calcualate the mean of a set of data.

Display

	A	B
1		X
2		3
3		4
4		12
5		10
6		9
7		___
8	NUM=	5
9	SUM=	38
10	MEAN=	7.6

$$\text{Mean} = \frac{\text{sum of data}}{\text{number of data}}$$

Formulas

	A	B
1		X
2		3
3		4
4		12
5		10
6		9
7		` ` ___
8	NUM=	@COUNT(B2..B6)
9	SUM=	@SUM(B2..B6)
10	MEAN=	+B9/B8

Steps for creating the model:

1. Enter labels as shown.
2. Enter data values in cells B2 through B6.
3. Enter @COUNT(B2..B6) in cell B8.
4. Enter the formulas for summing and averaging in cells B9 and B10 as shown.

Order: Column

You can expand this model to accommodate more data by inserting rows between rows 2 and 6. The ranges in the @COUNT and @SUM formulas will be expanded automatically.

EXAMPLE 2

Design a spreadsheet to find the mean of the following data:
8 scores of 98, 15 scores of 83, 23 scores of 72

We could use the spreadsheet model in Example 1. We would, however, have to make 46 entries. We will instead design a more efficient model for data like this, which we call grouped data.

Display

	A	B	C
1	F	X	FX
2	8	98	784
3	15	83	1245
4	23	72	1656
5			0
6			0
7			
8	NUM=		46
9	SUM =		3685
10	MEAN =		80.10869

Formulas

	A	B	C
1	F	X	FX
2	8	98	+A2*B2
3	15	83	+A3*B3
4	23	72	+A4*B4
5			+A5*B5
6			+A6*B6
7			
8	NUM =		@SUM(A2..A6)
9	SUM =		@SUM(C2..C6)
10	MEAN =		+C9/C8

Order: Column
Copy C2 Down: *RR*

Steps for creating the model:
1. Enter labels and data as shown.
2. Enter + A2*B2 in cell C2. Copy this formula down the column.
3. Enter the formulas for counting, summing, and averaging in cells C8, C9, and C10.

EXERCISES

1. Modify the model for Example 1 to allow for more data values. Then find the mean.
   a. {100, 99, 90, 85, 80, 75, 75}   **b.** {56, 78, 123, 77, 98, 22, 100, 120}

2. Find the mean for the grouped data.
   a. 18 scores of 99, 22 scores of 13, 30 scores of 27
   b. 1000 scores of 5, 250 scores of 8, 482 scores of 10, 522 scores of 9

3. The model for Example 2 can also be used to find weighted averages. Note that the "weights" need not be integers. Use the model to find a student's average if the teacher wants the first test to be 10% of the grade, the second test 40% of the grade, and the third test 50% of the grade.

	Test 1	Test 2	Test 3
Weight (f):	.1	.4	.5
Score (x):	80	90	100

4. A teacher gives 5 tests. Ann receives scores of 95, 90, 80, and 88 on the first four tests. Find the possible scores that Ann can get on the last test if she wants to have an average of 90 or better if
   a. all tests count the same.   **b.** the tests are weighted 10%, 10%, 20%, 20%, 40%.

BASIC Computer Projects

Each BASIC Computer Project presents one or more BASIC commands and a computer program using these commands. The project includes exercises in which the student is asked to modify the given program, and a section entitled "On Your Own," which suggests several related programs for the student to write and use on a computer.

Using the worksheets in succession, students receive an introduction to programming in BASIC. In addition, they will learn to create algorithms for a variety of mathematical manipulations.

We can use the PRINT statement in three different ways: to display any keyboard characters enclosed in quotation marks; to evaluate an arithmetic expression; and to display a blank line.

EXAMPLE

```
10   REM THE PRINT STATEMENT          Inserts explanatory remarks in a program.
20   PRINT ``SIMPLIFY EXPONENT FIRST''  Prints the words inside the quotes.
30   PRINT                             Displays a blank line.
40   PRINT ``12^2 / 3 = ''             Prints the characters inside the quotes.
50   PRINT 12^2 / 3                    Evaluates the expression.
60   END
```

EXERCISES

1.
```
10   REM EVALUATE EXPRESSIONS
20   PRINT ``A = 2   B = 5''
30   PRINT ``9A(B)^2 =''
40   _____
50   END
```
Write a statement for line 40 that will evaluate the expression in line 30, $9AB^2$, for $A = 2$, $B = 5$.

2.
```
10   REM EVALUATE EXPRESSIONS
20   PRINT ``A = 8   B = 10''
30   PRINT ``(A + 3*B)/5 =''
40   _____
50   END
```
Write a statement for line 40 that will evaluate the expression in line 30, $\dfrac{A + 3B}{5}$, for $A = 8$ and $B = 10$.

ON YOUR OWN

1. Write a program that will display and evaluate the following expressions:

$$10 + 3 \times 5$$
$$(9 - 3)^2$$
$$9 - 3^2$$

2. Write a program that will display and evaluate the following expressions.

$$4 + 124 \times 182 - 18$$
$$32 + 48 \times 13 \div 42$$
$$12 - 9 \div 2 \times 6$$

3. Write a program that will display and evaluate the expression $\dfrac{3X}{2Y + 1}$ for $X = 7$ and $Y = 3$.

4. Write a program that will display and evaluate the expressions $C + \dfrac{7}{5C^2}$ for $C = 82$.

5. Write a program that will display and evaluate the expressions $7A^6$ and $(7A)^6$ for $A = 4$.

6. Write a program that will display and evaluate the expression $9(18B + 8)$ for $B = 7$, $B = 20$, and $B = 412$.

Numeric Variables

We can use variables to name specific addresses in a computer's memory and store information in them. The computer will accept variable names of any length, but only the first two letters are significant. Variable names must begin with a letter.

EXAMPLE

```
10  REM AREA OF A TRIANGLE
20  LET H = 16          Stores the value 16 in an address named H.
30  LET B = 20          Stores the value 20 in an address named B.
40  LET A = (B * H)/2   Defines A as the value of (B * H)/2.
50  PRINT ``AREA = ''; A  Displays AREA = followed by the value of A. The semi-colon (;) forces
60  END                      the output for A on the same line as the words AREA = .
```

EXERCISES

1. Which of the following are not legal variable names?

```
X = 4
T3 = 7
3H = 2
AREA = 9
*B = 8
```

_____

2.
```
10   REM MANIPULATING A
       VARIABLE
20   LET Z = 4
30   LET Y = Z^2
40   LET X = Y / 2
50   LET W = X - 4
60   PRINT ``THE VALUE OF W IS
       ''; W
70   END
```
What is the output of this program?

_____

ON YOUR OWN

1. Write a program that uses the LET statement to find the square and cube of −5.4.

2. Use the LET and PRINT statements to find the area and circumference of a circle whose radius is 3.4 cm. Use 3.14159 for π($A = \pi r^2$ and $C = 2\pi r$).

3. Use the PRINT and LET statements to find the volume of a rectangular prism whose base area is 20 cm^2 and height is 6 cm (volume = area of base × height).

4. Use the LET and PRINT statements to find the total amount due on a 1 year loan of $4500 at 11.4% interest (interest = principal × rate × time).

5. Write a program that will find the total cost of a radio at $54.99, records at $26.75, and a cammera at $127.99. The sales tax for these purchases is 7%.

6. Write a program that will list the height in meters for 5 people. Compute and display the average height for the group.

String Variables

As with numeric variables, string variables can be manipulated in various ways. Names for string variables must begin with a letter and must end with a dollar sign ($). The characters assigned to a string variable must be enclosed in quotation marks.

EXAMPLE

```
10   REM USING STRING VARIABLES
20   LET A$ = ``AL''          Puts the string AL in a location named A$.
30   LET B$ = ``RA''          Puts the string RA in a location named B$.
40   LET C$ = ``GEB''         Puts the string GEB in a location named C$.
50   LET Z$ = A$ + C$ + B$    Defines Z$ as the values of A$ + B$ + C$.
60   PRINT Z$                 Displays the value of Z$ (ALGEBRA).
70   PRINT LEFT$(Z$,4)        Prints the leftmost 4 characters of Z$ (ALGE).
80   PRINT MID$(Z$,3,2)       Prints 2 characters of Z$, starting with letter 3 (GE).
90   END
```

EXERCISES

1.
```
10   REM STRINGS
20   LET H$ = ``HOUSES''
30   PRINT H$
40   _____
50   END
```
Write a statement for Line 40 that will output the letters USE from the string stored as H$.

2.
```
10   REM CONCATENATION
20   LET C$ = ``NIGHT''
30   LET X$ = ``MID''
40   _____
50   PRINT E$
60   END
```
The output is MIDNIGHT. Write the missing statement to produce this output.

ON YOUR OWN

1. Write a program that names the strings "A", "T", and "R" as three different variables and manipulates these variables to make three words.

2. Assign the word BULLETIN to a string variable. Use the LEFT$ and MID$ functions to print these words from BULLETIN: LET, TIN, IN, and BULL.

3. Store the sentence DO YOU HAVE SIX CHAIRS? as a single variable. Use the string functions to print the words YOU HAVE SIX HAIRS? from the string variable. Note: spaces count as characters in a string.

4. Write your first and last names as a single string with no space between them. Use the LEFT$ and MID$ functions to print your first name on one line and your last name beneath it.

5. Let A$ = "RE". Use five different variables to form words with the prefix RE.

6. Store the string "2,4,6,1,3,5,7" as a string variable. Use string functions to print the even numbers in this string under the title EVEN NUMBERS and the odd numbers under the title ODD NUMBERS.

Punctuation

We can use different forms of punctuation to format output in different ways. A comma (,) will force the output into three zones or columns. A semi-colon (;) will force two outputs on the same line. A colon (:) will allow us to concatenate two or more statements on one line, but these will be treated as separate statements by the computer.

EXAMPLE

```
10   REM PUNCTUATION
20   LET X = -2 : LET Y = 3
30   PRINT ``NUMBER'',``SQUARE'',``CUBE''
40   PRINT X,X^2,X^3
50   PRINT Y,Y^2,Y^3
60   PRINT ``(-2 × 3)^2 ='';

70   PRINT (-2 * 3)^2
```

Assigns values to X and Y.
Prints titles in three zones.
Prints the values of X, X^2, X^3.
Prints the values of Y, Y^2, Y^3.
Prints the equation and forces the output from line 70 on the same line.
Prints the value of the equation.

EXERCISES

1.
```
10   REM FIND DISTANCE
20   LET R = 55 LET T = 3.5
30   LET D = R * T
40   PRINT ``THE DISTANCE
     IS'';D
50   END
```
What punctuation mark should be used in line 20 to make the statement correct?

2.
```
10   REM FIND RATE
20   LET D = 150 : LET T = 3
30   PRINT ``DISTANCE''
     ``RATE'' ``TIME''
40   LET R = D/T
50   PRINT D R T
60   END
```
What punctuation mark should be used in lines 30 and 50 to align the output in three columns?

ON YOUR OWN

1. Write a program that will evaluate the square and the cube of the numbers 23, 34, and 48. Display your answers in three columns, with each given number in the first column.

2. Find the original amount borrowed if the total due was $4130 after one year at an interest rate of 18% per year. Display your solution on the same line as the statement THE ORIGINAL LOAN WAS.

3. Lisa's average for three algebra tests is 88%. Write a program to find her score on the third test if her first two grades were 76% and 89%. Use one line to list the variables for her first and second test scores.

4. Find the circumference of 3 circles if their diameters are 16, 8, and 14 cm. Display your answers under the column titles DIAMETER and CIRCUMFERENCE. Use the formula $C = \pi d$.

5. Use 5 statements, including REM and END to find and display the perimeter of a quadrilateral whose sides measure 17, 23, 19, and 11 cm.

6. Use 7 statements, including REM and END to find and print the values for 175% of 200, 450, 500, and 700.

Input Statements

We can use the INPUT statement to assign a value to a variable when the program is run. INPUT statements allow users to run the same program with different values for the variables. Use commas to separate the names of variables when more than one is used in a program.

EXAMPLE

```
10   REM AVERAGES
20   PRINT ``TYPE 3 SCORES, SEPARATED BY         Gives the user directions.
     A COMMA.''
30   INPUT A, B, C                               Sets up 3 variables: A, B, and C.
40   LET Z = (A + B + C)/3                       Computes the average of the scores.
50   PRINT ``THE AVERAGE SCORE IS ''; Z          Prints the statement and the average.
60   END
```

EXERCISES

1.
```
10   PRINT ``TYPE YOUR NAME.''
20   INPUT N$
30   PRINT ``TYPE THE YEAR AND
     YOUR AGE.''
40   _____
50   PRINT N$; ``, YOU WERE BORN
     IN''; Y - A
60   END
```
Write an INPUT statement for line 40.

2.
```
10   PRINT ``TYPE YOUR NAME AND
     TWO NUMBERS.''
20   _____
30   PRINT N$; ``, THE SUM OF
     YOUR NUMBERS IS ''; A + B
40   PRINT ``THE PRODUCT OF
     YOUR NUMBERS IS ''; A * B
50   END
```
Write an INPUT statement for line 20.

ON YOUR OWN

1. Write a program that allows the user to input a temperature in degrees Celsius. Convert this to degrees Fahrenheit with the formula $F = \frac{9}{5}C + 32$.

2. Find the average of five test scores typed in by the user. Display this number with the statement THE AVERAGE SCORE IS.

3. Write a program that will allow the user to input the length and width of a rectangle. Use this information to compute and to print the perimeter and area of the figure next to appropriate statements.

4. Write a program that asks the user to input his/her name, the distance traveled in kilometers, and the rate in kilometers per hour. Have the computer greet the user by name and inform him/her of the time needed to travel that distance at a rate given.

5. Write a program that instructs the user to input any even integer. Have the computer compute and display the sum of that integer and its consecutive even integer.

6. Write a program that asks the user to input the base and height of a triangle. Display the area of the triangle, then triple the length of the base and height and display the area of the new measurements.

Formatting Statements

We can format output by using the HTAB and VTAB commands. HTAB X will move the cursor horizontally and print the output X spaces from the left margin (0 − 39). VTAB Y will move the cursor vertically and print the output Y lines from the top of the screen (0 − 23). The HOME command clears the screen and positions the cursor at the upper left.

EXAMPLE

```
10   HOME
20   HTAB 17:VTAB 12
30   PRINT ``HELLO''
40   VTAB 22:PRINT ``PRESS RETURN''
50   INPUT R$
60   HOME
70   HTAB 15:VTAB 12
80   PRINT ``GOODBYE''
90   END
```

Clears the screen for new output.
Brings the cursor to line 12, horizontal space 17.
Prints HELLO at the current cursor position.
Prints this message at line 22 of the screen.
Accepts input from the user.
Clears all output from the screen.
Brings the cursor to line 12, horizontal space 20.
Prints GOODBYE at the current cursor position.

EXERCISES

1.
```
10   REM CENTER THE TITLE
20   HOME
30   _____
40   PRINT ``ALGEBRA''
50   END
```
Write two statements for line 30 that will center the output on the screen.

2.
```
20   PRINT ``INPUT 2 NUMBERS''
30   INPUT A,B
40   HTAB 5:VTAB 22:PRINT
     ``PRESS RETURN''
50   INPUT A$
60   _____
70   PRINT ``THE SUM OF '';
     A ; ``AND ''; B ;
     `` IS '';A+B
```
Write statements for line 60 that will clear the screen and center the output.

ON YOUR OWN

1. Write a program that will evaluate the following expressions for $A = 3$, $B = 5$, and $C = 10$. Display each expression and its solution on a clear screen.

$$(A + B)^2 + C \qquad (AB)^2(AC)^2 \qquad \frac{C^3 A}{B}$$

2. Write a program that allows the user to input his/her last name, first name, and middle initial. Use the appropriate string functions and punctuation to display the name as first name, middle initial, and last name in the center of the screen.

3. Write a program that will compute the sales tax at a rate of 6% on purchases totaling $197.00. Display the amount of sales tax on the tenth screen line. Then skip a line and display the total cost.

4. Write a program that allows the user to input a length for the side of a square. Compute and display the perimeter of the square. Ask the user to press RETURN. Compute and display the area of the square.

Read/Data Statements

We use the READ and DATA statements to assign values to variables. A GOTO statement will make the computer read each of the values listed as DATA until all the DATA is read. At this point, an OUT OF DATA statement will be displayed on the screen. Remember to separate variable names with a comma, and to place a comma between items in the DATA statement.

EXAMPLE

`10  REM AREA OF A RECTANGLE`	
`20  READ A, B`	Stores two consecutive variables as *A* and *B*.
`30 PRINT ``THE LENGTH IS ``; A`	Displays the value of *A*.
`40 PRINT ``THE WIDTH IS ``; B`	Displays the value of *B*.
`50 PRINT ``THE AREA IS ``; A*B`	Computes and displays the area of the figure.
`60  GOTO 20`	Sends the computer back to the READ statement.
`70  DATA 3, 10, 9, 5, 18, 4, 8, 6`	Contains the values for the variables.
`80  END`	

EXERCISES

1.
```
10   REM LIST NAMES AND SCORES
20   DATA BILL, 85, 79, ANN, 96,
     88
30   DATA JIM, 88, 94, BETH, 93,
     86
40   PRINT ``NAME``, ``MATH``,
     ``SCIENCE``
50   READ N$, X, Y
60   _____
70   GOTO 50
```
Write a statement for line 60 that will display the names and scores under the column headings.

2.
```
10   REM COMPUTE AVERAGES
20   _____
30   LET G=(A+B+C+D)/4
40   PRINT ``AVERAGE IS ``; G
50   GOTO 20
60   DATA 90, 70, 45, 65, 75,
     80, 80, 90
70   DATA 90, 90, 80, 90, 75,
     85, 95, 95
```
Write a statement for line 20 that will read and store four scores at a time.

ON YOUR OWN

1. Use the READ/DATA statement to evaluate the expression $(3C)^2 + 9C - 4$ for $C = -5, 3, 0.2,$ and 5.5.

2. Use the READ/DATA statement to find solutions to the equation $Q = (P + 5) - 7$ for $P = -3, 0.4, 11, 5.2,$ and -0.6.

3. Write a program with READ/DATA statements that will compute and display the areas of triangles whose base and height are 7 and 8.4, 9.3 and 0.9, 18.2 and 23, and 6.4 and 3.8.

4. Evaluate $5X^2 + 3XY - Y$ for $X = 0.2, 2, -2, 2.2$ and $Y = 0.5, 5, -5,$ and 5.5. Display the values of *X* and *Y* and the result of each evaluation.

5. Maria's scores were 96, 94 and 98. Jeff's were 92, 89 and 93. Sara's scores were 75, 85 and 95. Jason's were 83, 68 and 72. Write a program which stores these values in DATA statements and computes the average for each person. Display the average with the student's name.

6. Write a program that will raise each of the following numbers to the 4th, 5th, and 6th powers. Display these values in three columns with appropriate titles.
DATA $-2, 0.4, 5, 10, -0.3, 7$

If . . . Then Statements

We use IF . . . THEN statements to make a decision. If the assertion is true, the computer executes the THEN clause. If the assertion is false, the computer executes the next line in the program. The symbols used in assertions are $<, >, =, <>, <=, >=$.

EXAMPLE

```
10   PRINT ``TYPE A NUMBER.''
20   INPUT P
30   IF P > 10 THEN 70
40   IF P < 10 THEN 90
50   PRINT ``YOUR NUMBER IS 10''
60   GOTO 100
70   PRINT P; ``IS GREATER THAN 10''
80   GOTO 100
90   PRINT P; ``IS LESS THAN 10''
100  END
```

Displays a message to the user.
Sets up a variable P.
Tests P for $P > 10$.
Tests P for $P < 10$.
The default message for $P = 10$.
Executes line 100.
The message for $P > 10$.
Executes line 100.
The message for $P < 10$.

EXERCISES

1.
```
10   READ A,B
20   _____
30   PRINT A; ``IS GREATER
     THAN ''; B
40   GOTO 60
50   PRINT A; ``IS LESS
     THAN '' ; B
60   GOTO 10
70   DATA 0.02, 0.04, -4, -3,
     2.01, -2.01
80   END
```
Write a statement for line 20 that will test if the value of A is less than the value of B.

2.
```
10   PRINT ``ENTER THE SUM OF
     -2.45, AND 4.5''
20   INPUT Z
30   _____
40   PRINT ``THE SUM IS'';
     -2.45 + 4.5
50   GOTO 70
60   PRINT ``RIGHT!''
70   END
```
Write a statement for line 30 that will test whether the user's input is correct.

ON YOUR OWN

1. Write a program that allows the user to input any number. Use IF . . . THEN statements to determine if the number is positive, negative or zero. Display a message for each condition.

2. Write a program to find which of the following numbers are solutions of $0.5(A + 5) < 0.2(3 + A)$.

$$-100, -30, -9, -7, -6.3, -6.5,$$
$$-6, -5.5, 0$$

3. Write a program that allows the user to input two numbers. Display a message which asks the user whether he/she wants to see the sum or the product of these numbers and display the result.

4. Allow the user to input any 5 positive integers. Compute the average of these numbers, and display the message YOU RECEIVED A PASSING GRADE if the average is ≥ 75.

5. Write a program that allows the user to input any integer. If the integer is negative, display it and its absolute value. If the integer is positive, inform the user that it is positive.

6. Write a program using READ/DATA to show that the expressions $(X + 1)(X - 1)$ and $X^2 - 1$ are equal for 6 different values of X.

Functions

We can use any of the built-in functions to help us perform algebraic operations. Some of the functions are: RND(1)—generates random numbers between 0 and 1 (not including 0 and 1); INT(X)—generates the integer value of a number less than or equal to X; ABS(X)—generates the absolute value of X; SQR(X)—generates the square root of X.

EXAMPLE

10	LET X = 0	Sets the value of X to 0.
20	IF X > 10 THEN GOTO 60	Tests to see if X > 10.
30	PRINT X , INT (X) , SQR(X)	Prints X, the integer value of X, the square root of X.
40	X = X + 0.5	Increments the value of X by 0.05.
50	GOTO 20	Sends computer to line 20.
60	END	

EXERCISES

1.
```
10   REM ABSOLUTE VALUE OF SUMS
20   READ A , B
30   _____
40   GOTO 20
50   DATA -3 , 4 , -7 , -2 , -9 , 8 ,
     3 , -1
60   END
```
Write a statement for line 30 that will display the absolute value of the sum of *A* and *B*.

2.
```
10   REM RANDOM NUMBERS
20   READ X
30   Y = INT(X * RND(1)) + 1
40   PRINT Y
50   DATA 9 , 45 , 32 , 76 , 89 , 90
60   GOTO 20
70   END
```
Read the program carefully. What is the largest integer this program will generate?

ON YOUR OWN

1. Write a program that will print the integers from 1 to 10 and their square roots.

2. Use the RND and INT functions to write a number guessing game for integers between 1 and 25. Give the user one of three different messages after each guess: YOUR GUESS IS TOO HIGH; YOUR GUESS IS TOO LOW; or THAT'S IT!

3. Write a program that allows the user to enter any two negative numbers. Have the computer compute and print the absolute value of the difference between these numbers.

4. Write a program that will compute and display the sum of the square roots of the numbers from 25 to 34.

5. Write a program that allows the user to input any three digit numbers. Use the INT function to compute and print the factors for this number.

6. Write a program that will compute and print the value for 100 times the square root of any integer input by the user.

For . . . Next Statements

We can use FOR . . . NEXT statements to instruct the computer to repeat a sequence of instructions. We can also use FOR . . . NEXT statements to create a pause in a program (a delay loop), or to increment a series of numbers with the STEP command.

EXAMPLE

```
10   FOR X = 1 TO 5 STEP .2
20   PRINT X
30   NEXT X
40   END
```

Increments X by 0.2 for X = 1 to 10.
Prints the current value of X.
Retrieves the next value of X.

EXERCISES

1.
```
10   REM DECREASING INTEGERS
20   FOR A = 10 TO 0 STEP -2
30   PRINT A
40   NEXT A
50   END
```
Which numbers will be output from this program?

2.
```
10   REM SQUARES
20   FOR C = 1 TO 10
30   _____
40   NEXT C
50   END
```
Write a statement for line 30 that will display C, C^2 and C^3.

ON YOUR OWN

1. Use a FOR . . . NEXT loop to compute and print the numbers from 20 to 30, their squares, and their cubes.

2. Write a number guessing game for integers between 1 and 25 so that the user can make three guesses before the computer's number is displayed.

3. Use the FOR . . . NEXT and READ/DATA statements to convert 5 temperatures in degrees Fahrenheit to degrees Celsius. Use this formula.

$$C = \frac{5}{9}F - 32$$

4. Use the FOR . . . NEXT and READ/DATA statements to compute the volume and area of 6 cubes whose edges measure 3, 4.2, 2, 3, 8, and 9.4 cm. Use the formulas $V = e^3$ for volume and $A = 6e^2$ for area.

5. Use the FOR . . . NEXT loop with the numbers 2 to 20 to show that the sum of any two even numbers is an even number. Print the algorithms and create a pause before each is displayed on the screen.

6. Write a program that will compute and display the sum of the integer values of the square roots of the integers from 1 to 10.

Low Resolution Graphics

We can create low resolution graphics by plotting horizontal lines, vertical lines, and points as ordered pairs on a 0-39 *X*-axis and a 0-39 *Y*-axis. The statements for low resolution graphics are:

GR	Sets the low resolution graphics screen.
COLOR = N	Sets a color from 0 to 15.
PLOT X , Y	Plots a point at the intersection of the *X*- and *Y*-coordinates.
HLIN X , X AT Y	Plots a horizontal line from the first to the second *X*-coordinate at the *Y*-coordinate.
VLIN Y , Y AT X	Plots a vertical line from the first to the second *Y*-coordinate at the *X*-coordinate.

EXAMPLE

10	REM COLOR SCREEN	
20	GR ·	Sets the low resolution graphics screen.
30	COLOR = 1	Sets color 1.
40	FOR Y = 0 TO 39	Tells the number of times the loop will be executed.
50	HLIN 0 , 39 AT Y	Plots a horizontal line at each *Y* value.
60	NEXT Y	Increments the value of *Y* by 1.
70	END	

EXERCISES

1. 30   PLOT 20 , 10
This statement will plot a point at the intersection of _____ on the *X*-axis and _____ on the *Y*-axis.

2. 50   HLIN 5 , 10 AT 30
This statement will display a _____ from point 5 to point 10 on the _____ axis at point 30 on the _____ axis.

3. 90   VLIN 0 , 25 AT 5
This statement will display a _____ from point 0 to point _____ on the *Y*-axis at point _____ on the *X*-axis.

4. 20   FOR X = 1 TO 10
30   PLOT X , 3
40   NEXT X
These statements will display a series of ten ordered pairs from 1, 3, to _____.

5. 10   REM PLOT A WHITE POINT
20   GR
40   PLOT 12 , 3
50   END
Which statement is missing from the above program?

6. 10   REM PLOT RANDOM COLOR
           POINTS
20   GR
40   COLOR = C
50   PLOT 2 , 3 : PLOT 4 , 8 : PLOT
           1 , 1
60   END
Which statement is missing from the above program?

ON YOUR OWN

1. Revise the sample program by using an IF , , , THEN loop to color the graphics screen yellow.

2. Write a program which uses a FOR , , , NEXT loop to plot a diagonal line from the 0, 0 to the 39, 39 coordinates.

3. Use the INT and RND functions to plot horizontal lines in a random selection of the 16 low resolution COLORS.

4. Write a program which uses the INT and RND functions to plot a series of random points in random colors on your screen.

Animating Low Resolution Graphics

We can animate low resolution graphics by using a series of instructions to first draw and then erase a figure within a loop. Erasing a figure is accomplished by drawing the figure in the same colors as the background color. Delay loops are an important part of animating since they slow down the movement of a figure enough to be perceived by the human eye.

EXAMPLE

```
10   REM ANIMATE A POINT          Sets the low resolution graphics mode.
20   GR                           Sets X-coordinate to 0 to 39.
30   FOR X = 0 TO 39              Sets Y-coordinate to 20.
40   Y = 20                       Sets color 15.
50   COLOR = 15                   Plots a point at X, Y.
60   PLOT X , Y                   Generates a pause.
70   FOR T = 1 TO 50:NEXT T       Sets color 0.
80   COLOR = 0                    "Erases" the original point.
90   PLOT X , Y                   Generates a pause.
100  FOR T = 1 TO 50:NEXT T       Increments the value of the X-coordinate.
110  NEXT X
120  END
```

EXERCISES

1.
```
10   REM VERTICAL ANIMATION
20   GR
30   FOR Y = 0 TO 39: X = 5
40   COLOR = 1 : PLOT X , Y
50   FOR K = 1 TO 80: NEXT K
60   _____
70   PLOT X , Y
80   FOR K = 1 TO 80: NEXT K
90   NEXT Y
```

Write a statement for line 60 which will complete the animation program.

2.
```
10   REM LINE ANIMATION
20   GR : FOR Y = 0 TO 39
30   COLOR = 6:HLIN 0 , 10 AT Y
40   FOR J = 1 TO 80:NEXT J
50   COLOR = 0
60   _____
70   FOR J = 1 TO 80: NEXT J
80   NEXT Y
```

Write a statement for line 60 which will complete the animation program.

ON YOUR OWN

1. Write a program which will display a red point at coordinates 0, 0 and animate it to coordinates 39, 39.

2. Revise the program you wrote for problem 1 so that the point starts at coordinates 39, 39 and ends at coordinates 0, 0.

3. Write a program which will draw an orange horizontal line at the top of your screen and drop it to the bottom of the screen.

4. Write a program which will animate a vertical line from the right to the left side of your screen.

5. Write a program which will animate two points on your screen. The first should start at the top and move to the bottom. Then the second should start at the bottom and move to the top of your screen.

6. Revise the program in problem 5 so that two lines are animated in the same manner.

High Resolution Graphics

We can use the high resolution graphics statements to draw more precise lines on a plane with 280 points on the *X*-axis and 193 points on the *Y*-axis. The high resolution graphics statements are:

HGR	Sets the high resolution graphics screen.
HCOLOR = IN	Sets a high resolution color from 0 to 7.
HPLOT X , Y	Plots a point at the intersection of the *X*- and *Y*-coordinates.
HPLOT X1 , Y1 TO X2 , Y2	Plots a continuous line from the first set of *X*, *Y* coordinates to the second.

EXAMPLE

```
10   REM DRAW A RECTANGLE
20   HGR                        Sets the high resolution graphics screen.
30   HCOLOR = 3                 Sets the color.
40   HPLOT 3 , 10 TO 80 , 10 TO   Plots a continuous line from one set of ordered pairs to the next.
     80 , 50 TO 3 , 50 TO 3 , 10
```

EXERCISES

1. 40   FOR Y = 1 TO 50
    50   HPLOT 10 , Y
    60   NEXT Y
These statements will display a series of _____ points from the 10,1 coordinate to the _____ coordinate.

2. 10   REM DRAW A RIGHT TRIANGLE
    30   HCOLOR = 3
    40   HPLOT 0 , 0 TO 0 , 100 TO
        279 , 100 TO 0 , 0
    50   END
Which statement is missing from the above program?

_____

3. 10   REM DRAW A SHAPE
    20   HGR : HCOLOR = 3
    30   HPLOT 10 , 10 TO 20 , 10 TO
        20 , 20 TO 10 , 20 TO 10 , 10
    40   END
Which shape will this program display?

_____

4. 10   REM PLOT LINES
    20   HGR : HCOLOR = 5
    30   FOR N = 1 TO 5
    40   X = INT (100 * RND (1))
    50   Y = INT (100 * RND (1))
    60   HPLOT X , Y
    70   NEXT N
    80   END
How many random points will this program generate?

_____

ON YOUR OWN

1. Use a FOR . . . NEXT loop to display a graph for the linear equation $Y = 2X + 5$. Use the values 0 to 50 for *X*.

2. Revise exercise 6, listed above, so that 100 random points will be generated in random colors.

3. Write a program which uses the READ / DATA statements to display 6 quadrilaterals of different sizes on your screen.

4. Design a display of your choice by plotting a series of ordered pairs. Use the READ / DATA statements to plot the coordinates on your screen.

Coin, Age and Integer Problems

We can set up algorithms so the computer can solve word problems. Each expression must be developed for computer solution, which may involve setting up the equation in a way different from the standard solution for a problem.

EXAMPLE

```
10   REM TWO INTEGERS HAVE A SUM
15   REM OF 46 AND DIFFERENCE OF 12
20   PRINT ``X + Y = 46''              Displays first equation.
30   PRINT ``X - Y = 12''              Displays second equation.
40   PRINT ``2X = 58''                 Displays partial solution.
50   LET X = 58/2                      Solves for X.
60   LET Y = 46 - X                    Solves for Y.
70   IF X - Y = 12 THEN PRINT ``X = '';X :    Prints values of X and Y.
     PRINT ``Y = '';Y
80   END
```

EXERCISES

1. Write two statements which will display the equations for the following problem: The sum of two numbers is 16 and their difference is 2.

2. Write a statement which will display a partial solution for the equations you printed in problem 1.

ON YOUR OWN

1. Write a program which will find two numbers whose sum is 26. One number is 1 less than twice the value of the other.

2. The sum of Maria's and Jeff's ages is 25. Jeff is 5 years older than Maria. Write a program to find the age for each.

3. Write a program to find the sum and difference for any two numbers input by the user.

4. Write a program which asks the user to input two ages. Find the sum and difference of the ages and use this information to display a word problem for these ages.

5. Write a program to find the number of dimes and quarters Kelly has if her coins total $1.95 and she has two more dimes than quarters.

6. Ask the user to input the number of nickels and the number of dimes. Print the total amount of money and the total number of coins. Use this information to print a problem for these facts.

Radical Expressions/Pythagorean Theorem

We can use the SQR function of the computer to solve problems involving radicals, such as problems involving the Pythagorean theorem. Remember to use the appropriate number of parentheses to set up equations for computer solution.

EXAMPLE

```
10   REM SIMPLIFY A RADICAL
20   PRINT ''20 SQR(3/5) + 12 SQR (5/3) = ''
30   PRINT 20 * (SQR(3/5)) + 12 * (SQR(5/3))
40   END
```

Prints the expression as shown.
Evaluates the expression.
Note how the parentheses are used.

EXERCISES

1. After applying the Pythagorean theorem, the length of the hypotenuse was found to be 5 m. Write a statement which will display the length of the hypotenuse in cm.

2. Write a statement which will simplify the following radical expression.

$$(7 + 2\sqrt{3})(7 - 2\sqrt{3})$$

ON YOUR OWN

1. Write a program which will allow the user to input the length of two legs of a right triangle. Have the computer display the length of the hypotenuse.

2. Write a program which will prove that a triangle with legs 3 cm and 16 cm, and a hypotenuse of 34 cm is not a right triangle. Display your solution as whole number values.

3. Write a program to find the area of a triangle whose base is 607.2 cm and height is 7.2 cm.

4. Write a program to find the length of one leg of a right triangle if the hypotenuse is 96 cm and leg is 12 cm.

5. Baseball diamonds are 90 feet on a side. Write a program which will compute and display the perimeter, area, and the distance from first to third base (the diagonal) of the playing field.

6. A 34-foot ladder touches the wall of a building 30 feet above the ground. Write a program which will compute and display the distance from the base of the wall to the foot of the ladder.

Graphing Functions

We can use the high resolution graphics screen to graph functions. DEF FN $F(X)$ defines functions. DEF FN $F(X) = 3*X^2 - 1$ defines the function $F(X) = 3X^2 - 1$. DEF FN $G(X) = ABS(2*X - 1)$ defines the function $G(X) = |2X - 1|$.

EXAMPLE

```
1   REM FUNCTION GRAPHER
10  DEF FN F(X) = 3*X^2 - 1
20  X0 = 135: Y0 = 100

30  HGR2
40  REM DRAW AXES
50  HCOLOR = 3
60  HPLOT 0,Y0 TO 279,Y0
70  HPLOT X0,0 TO X0,191
80  REM PLOT FUNCTION
90  HCOLOR = 3
100 FOR X1 = 0 TO 279 STEP .5
110 X = (X1 - X0)/10
120 Y = FN F(X)
130 Y1 = Y0 - 10*Y
140 IF(Y1 >=) AND (Y1 <= 191)
    THEN HPLOT X1,Y1
150 NEXT X1
160 END
```

Defines the function to be graphed.

Sets the origin of the axes to the point (135,100) on the computer screen.

Draws the y-axis.
Draws the x-axis.

Increments the values of X^1.
Places the value of x on the screen in relation to the origin.
Determines the value of Y for the defined function.
Places the value of y on the screen in relation to the origin.
Plots (x,y) in relation to the origin if not off the screen.

EXERCISES

1. Modify the sample program so that it will graph the function $g(x) = |x - 2|$.

2. Modify the sample program so that the graph of the function will be more dense.

_____   _____

ON YOUR OWN

1. Write a program that will graph the following two functions on the same axes.

$$f(x) = |x - 2| \quad g(x) = |x + 2|$$

2. Write a program that will graph the following functions on the same axes.

$$f(x) = |3x - 2| \quad g(x) = |-3x - 2|$$

3. Write a program that will graph the following functions on the same axes.

$$f(x) = x^2 + 3x + 1$$
$$g(x) = x^2 - 3x - 1$$

4. Write a program that will graph the following functions on the same axes.

$$f(x) = x^3 + 2x^2 - 5x - 6$$
$$g(x) = -x^3 - 2x^2 + 5x + 6$$

Quadratic Equations

We can write programs to solve quadratic equations in the form $AX^2 + BX + C = 0$. Use the SQR function to translate this form of equation into the form $X = \dfrac{-B \pm \sqrt{B^2 - 4AC}}{2A}$ for easier solution.

EXAMPLE

```
10   REM SOLVE X^2 + 14X + 45 = 0
20   REM SOLVE X^2 + 10X + 9 = 0
30   READ A,B,C,                        Reads values of A, B, C.
40   IF (B^2) - (4 * A * 2) < 0 THEN 90  Tests for real numbers.
50   LET Z1 = (-B + SQR (B^2-4*A*C))/(2*A)  Finds one solution.
60   LET Z2 = (-B - SQR (B^2-4*A*C))/(2*A)  Finds second solution.
70   PRINT ``THE SOLUTIONS ARE '' ; Z1;   Displays solutions.
     ``AND'' ; Z2
80   GOTO 30                           Branches to line 30.
90   PRINT ``NO REAL NUMBER SOLUTIONS''  Message for line 40.
100  GOTO 30                           Branches to line 30.
110  DATA 1,14,45,1,10,9               Values for A,B,C.
120  END
```

EXERCISES

```
10   REM SOLVE X^2 - X + 3 = 0          80   PRINT ``NO REAL NUMBER
20   A = 1 : B = 1 : C = 3                   SOLUTIONS''
30   _____                         90   END
40   S1 = (-B + SQR(B^2 -
     4*A*C))/(2*A)
50   _____
60   PRINT ``THE SOLUTIONS
     ARE'' ; S1; ``AND'' S2
70   GOTO 90
```

Write the missing statements for lines 30 and 50 in order to find the solution to the quadratic equation.

1. _____

2. _____

ON YOUR OWN

1. Write a program which uses $READ/DATA$ statements to solve the following.

$$3X^2 + X - 1 = 0$$
$$X^2 + 2X - 24 = 0$$

2. Write a program to solve the following.

$$X^2 - 8X + 15 = 0$$
$$3X^2 - 6X + 1 = 0$$
$$5X^2 + 5X - 1 = 0$$

3. Write a program to solve the following quadratic equations. Use $READ/DATA$ statements to store the values of A, B, and C.

$$9X^2 - 4 = 0$$
$$8X^2 - 3 = 0$$

4. Write a program to solve the following quadratic equations. If an equation has no real number solution, print the equations with the message "HAS NO REAL NUMBER SOLUTION".

$$X^2 + 2X - 2 = 0$$
$$2X^2 + X + 3 = 0$$
$$3X^2 - 12 = 0$$

5. Write a program to solve.
A number is 18 greater than another number. The product of the two numbers is 180. What are the numbers?

6. Write a program to solve.
The area of a rectangle is 12 cm². Its perimeter is 11 cm. What is the length and width of the rectangle?

Compound Interest Problems

We can use the computer to generate solutions to compound interest problems. The solutions can show the financial growth for various amounts of principal invested. The FOR . . . NEXT loop is an efficient way to solve these problems. Use the formula $A = P(1 + R)^T$.

EXAMPLE

```
10   REM COMPOUND INTEREST
20   LET R = .15
30   LET T = 2
40   FOR P = 200 TO 215
50   LET S = P*(1 + R)^T
60   PRINT P; ''WILL YIELD'' ; S
70   NEXT P
```

Sets a variable for the interest rate.

Sets a variable for the time.

Sets range for amount of principal.

Finding the principal plus the compound interest.

EXERCISES

1. The following statement was included in a program to determine the amount of an investment after the interest was compounded for 3 years:

   $$50 A = P(1 + R)^T$$

   How would you write a FOR . . . NEXT loop to see the effects of the interest on $500, $550, $600, and $650?

2. Write a statement for a program which uses the formula

   $$S = P(1 + R)^T$$

   to find the total return on an investment. The statement should show the effects of the following rates of interest: 11%, 13%, 15%, and 17%.

ON YOUR OWN

1. Write a program to show the return on an investment of $750 for 24 years at 0.7% interest a month.

2. Modify the program in problem 1 to show the effects of the interest rate on possible investments of $800 to $1400 in increments of $100.

3. James wants to get the best possible return on his savings of $2000. Write a program to show the effects of the interest rates of 8.5%, 8.75%, and 12.9% on his savings after three years.

4. Linda's bankbook showed a balance of $3763.20 after 12% interest on her deposit was compounded for 2 years. Write a program which will compute and print the amount of her original deposit.

5. Three people each invested $500. Show the amount each received if the first invested at 13.2% for 3 years; the second at 12% for 5 years; and the third for 10.75% for 8 years.

6. Revise problem 5 to show the effects if the length of time of the investment was doubled for each person. Use appropriate PRINT statements for each situation.

Trigonometric Functions

We can use the trigonometric functions to evaluate angle functions. The trigonometric functions are: SIN(X)—to find the sine of an angle; COS(X)—to find the cosine of an angle; and TAN(X)—to find the tangent of an angle. Remember that computers measure angles in radians, rather than degrees. One degree is equal to $\frac{\pi}{180}$ radians.

EXAMPLE

```
10   REM LIST MEASURES OF ANGLES
15   REM AND THEIR SINE VALUES
20   PRINT ''DEGREES'' ''SINE''
30   LET R = 3.14159/180
40   FOR D = 1 TO 15
50   PRINT D, SIN(D * R)
60   NEXT D
70   END
```

Prints two column headings.
Converts degrees to radians.
Sets the range of values for degrees.
Prints the values of angles and sines.
Increments the value of the angles.

EXERCISES

1. Modify the sample program by changing lines 20 and 50 so the measure of the angles will be listed in radians as well as degrees.

2. Modify the sample program by changing lines 20 and 50 so the tangent value will be listed for each angle.

ON YOUR OWN

1. Use the appropriate trigonometric functions to compute and display the sine and cosine values for angles measuring 10 to 100 degrees in increments of 10 degrees.

2. Modify the program you wrote for problem 1 to compute and print the tangent values for angles measuring 10 to 180 degrees in increments of 10 degrees.

3. Two angles of a right triangle measure 45 and 90 degrees. The hypotenuse is 20 cm long. Write a program to compute and print the measure of the third angle and the length of the other sides.

4. Use READ/DATA statements to modify the program you wrote for problem 3. Have the new program compute and print the measure of the third angle and the length of the two unknown sides for two triangles whose measures are:

   Angles: 65°, 90°.   Hypotenuse: 30.
   Angles: 80°, 90°.   Hypotenuse: 60.

5. Write a program which allows the user to input the measure of any angle of a right triangle. Have the computer print the measure of the angle, and its sine, cosine, and tangent values.

6. Write a program which will display the measure of the third angle and the length of the two sides. Allow the user to input the measure of one angle and length of one side.

Simulation with a Computer

We can use a computer program to simulate events such as tossing a coin, or rolling a die. Most programs of this type make use of the random number generator that is a BASIC command. RND (1) will cause the computer to produce a random number between 0 and 1. Since it is often preferable to have the computer pick random integers instead of long random decimals, we can use the RND with the INT function. INT(X) finds the largest integer that is not greater than X. INT(N * RND(1) + A generates a random integer, where N is the number of integers in the set, and A is the lowest integer.

EXAMPLE

```
10   REM DIE SIMULATION
15   LET S = 6                              Sets number of sides of die.
20   PRINT ``HOW MANY TIMES TO ROLL DIE?''
30   INPUT N                                Input number of times to roll die.
40   PRINT ``HOW MANY TRIALS?''
50   INPUT T                                Input number of trials desired.
60   FOR J = 1 TO T
70   FOR I = 1 TO N
80   F = INT(S*RND(1) + 1)                  Assigns to F a random number from 1 to 6.
90   PRINT F;
100  NEXT I
110  PRINT
120  NEXT J
130  END
```

EXERCISES

1. Change one line in the above program so that the "die" will have 8 sides instead of 6 sides.

2. What does line 110 do for the program? (Delete this line and RUN the program if necessary.)

ON YOUR OWN

1. Write a program that will simulate tossing a coin.

2. Write a program that will generate 20 random numbers from 1 to 30.

3. Write a program that will generate 20 random numbers from 10 to 30.

4. Write a program that will simulate combinations of boys and girls for 20 families with 4 children. (Hint: Let "1" represent a boy and "2' represent a girl.)

CALCULATOR 1

1. 20 **2.** 5228 **3.** 89.8 **4.** 22.6 **5.** 8.07
6. 53.783 **7.** 100 **8.** 13.278 **9.** 0
10. 88 **11.** 90
Answers for 12-15 may vary. Answers are given for the T1-34, a calculator with 10-digit display and 112 digit memory that rounds the last digit in the memory.
12. 10 **13.** 12,345,678.12 **14.** 0.1235, 12 digits
15. 1,111,111,112; yes

CALCULATOR 2

1. 1024 **2.** 7744 **3.** 68.921 **4.** 0.281
5. 11,390,625 **6.** 74.712 **7.** 788,544 **8.** 277
9. 44.983 **10.** 9797.322 **11.** 63,753.4208 in.
12. 63,360 in. **13.** 1.006 mi **14.** $3^{16} = 43,046,721$
15. 2.704813829 **16.** 1 **17.** 0.366032341
18. No; if it is 1, it stays the same; if it is smaller than 1, it gets smaller.

CALCULATOR 3

1. 8 **2.** 12.842 **3.** 20.5 **4.** 5 **5.** 82.1 **6.** 22.2
7. 0.239 **8.** 3.606 **9.** 1.552 **10.** 1044
11. 1296.539 **12.** 371.224 **13.** 400.7
14. 0.8 **15.** 28,638.706 **16.** 31.5
17. Answers may vary. The T1-34 can handle 6 pending operations.

CALCULATOR 4

1. 12.111 **2.** 580.617 **3.** 5891.601 **4.** 341.322
5. $2.70 **6.** $0.03 **7.** $1944.14 **8.** $91.54
9. 45,819.6 **10.** 46,144.6 **11.** 46,422.0 **12.** 46,539.0

CALCULATOR 5

1. 0.2 **2.** 4.875 **3.** 0.75 **4.** 0.6875 **5.** 15.25
6. 22.9 **7.** 0.375 **8.** 0.0002
9. 0.32
0.3
>
10. 0.14
0.15
<
11. 0.1875
0.2
<
12. 0.111111111 **13.** 0.444444444 **14.** 33.33333333
15. 0.727272727 **16.** 0.636363636 **17.** 18.18181818
18. 0.131313131 **19.** 0.414141414 **20.** 0.505050505
21. The calculator rounds up the final digit in the display if the next digit is 5 or greater.
22. The decimal will consist of the numerator repeating continually.
23. $\frac{105}{999}$ and $\frac{8642}{9999}$

CALCULATOR 6

1. −57 **2.** −214 **3.** 484 **4.** 1294 **5.** 3.01
6. −997 **7.** 170.7 **8.** 0.625 **9.** 74.8
10. 104.6 **11.** Yes **12.** No
13.

Presley	Napoleon	King	Lincoln	You
1935	1769	1929	1809	Answers will vary.
5391	9671	9291	9081	Answers will vary.
−3456	−7902	−7362	−7272	Answers will vary.
−6543	−2097	−2637	−2727	Answers will vary.
−9999	−9999	−9999	−9999	−9999

14. They are not always the same, although −9999 is the most common result.

CALCULATOR 7

1. $0.\overline{4}$ (repeats) **2.** 0.504 (terminates)
3. 0.075 (terminates) **4.** 0.25 (terminates)
5. $0.\overline{51}$ (repeats) **6.** 0.0845 (terminates)
7. 0.285714 **8.** 0.428571 **9.** 0.571428
10. 0.714285
11. Each product contains the same digits in the same order.
12. 0.999999
13. Answers may vary. More sophisticated calculators will give the answer 1. Less sophisticated calculators will give 0.999999 as the answer. Note that 0.142857 is only an approximation of 1/7.
14. 2/9 **15.** 9/33 **16.** 83/99 **17.** 197/333

CALCULATOR 8

1. 0.125 **2.** 1000 **3.** −0.0025 **4.** 0.75 **5.** −0.07
6. $2.\overline{6}$ **7.** $x = 14$ **8.** $k = -0.35$ **9.** $m = 13.2$
10. $p = -0.087$
11. Error; $\frac{1}{x} = \frac{1}{0}$ and division by 0 is not possible.
12. The original number appears. **13.** x **14.** 0.5
15. 1 and −1 **16.** 78 **17.** 78
18. Answers may vary. Generally, division is preferable because fewer steps are required.

CALCULATOR 9

1. 557.5 cm² **2.** 15.2 h **3.** 442.4 yd **4.** 0.085
5. 3.141592654 **6.** 237.79 in.² **7.** 9.55 in.

CALCULATOR 10

1. 264 **2.** 37.8 **3.** 2 **4.** 150 **5.** 293.76
6. 0.0924 **7.** Yes **8.** Yes **9.** Yes **10.** No
11. Yes **12.** No

CALCULATOR 11

1. 18.8% **2.** 72.9% **3.** 160% **4.** 530.88 **5.** 91.6%
6. $45.58 **7.** 570 **8.** $473 **9.** $31.48
10. $25,467.75 **11.** Less
12. Final price is less than original.

CALCULATOR 12

1. $2797, $2942, $3087, $3232, $3377
2. 252; 1512; 9072; 54,432; 326,592
3. 10,485,760; 3,276,800; 1,024,000; 320,000; 100,000
4. Yes **5.** No **6.** Yes **7.** No **8.** Yes **9.** Yes
10. No **11.** No **12.** 1666 **13.** 6777

CALCULATOR 13

1. 3125 **2.** 5.160 **3.** 625 **4.** 248,185.7
5. 24,619.083 **6.** 7.594 **7.** 0.658 **8.** 3,048,625
9. 1 and −1 alternate; odd powers of −1 = −1, even powers = +1
10. −1 **11.** positive **12.** 65,536
13. −16,807 **14.** −30,517.578
15. Answers may vary; $2^{22} = 4,194,304$
16. Answers may vary; $2^{-22} \approx 0.0000002$

CALCULATOR 14

1. $1.192092895 \times 10^{16}$ **2.** $8.589934592 \times 10^{-57}$
3. $1.433536083 \times 10^{-10}$ **4.** $-6.195134677 \times 10^{71}$
5. 1.616292×10^{39} **6.** $2.293235712 \times 10^{9}$
7. $5.274134309 \times 10^{19}$
8. Answers may vary. $9,999,999,999 \times 10^{99}$
9. 69 on most calculators **10.** 3.0295×10^{9} times
11. $4000 **12.** $2,000,000

CALCULATOR 15

1. 0 **2.** 255 **3.** 2628 **4.** 18,913 **5.** −104.254
6. 4149.997 **7.** 51 ft **8.** 86 ft **9.** 100 ft
10. 96 ft and 96 ft; it reaches its high point between 2 sec and 3 sec
11. 0 ft; the ball has fallen back to the ground
12. 221.671 cm² **13.** 886.683 cm² **14.** 2482.713 cm³
15. $3350 **16.** $9350 **17.** $7250 **18.** No

CALCULATOR 16

	n	2	3	5	9	11
1.	8613	no	2871	no	957	783
2.	4845	no	1615	969	no	no
3.	67,232	33,616	no	no	no	6112
4.	36,630	18,315	12,210	7326	4070	3330
5.	19,427	no	no	no	no	no
6.	13,155	no	4385	2631	no	no
7.	29,337	no	9779	no	no	2667

8. 22 × 751 **9.** 15 × 1409 **10.** 33 × 971
11. 55 × 503 **12.** 45 × 821 or 15 × 2463
13. 27 × 1151

CALCULATOR 17

1. Yes **2.** No **3.** No **4.** Yes **5.** No **6.** Yes
7. Yes **8.** Yes **9.** Yes **10.** No **11.** Yes
12. 17 **13.** 3 **14.** 25 **15.** 62 **16.** 31

CALCULATOR 18

1. −72
   −36
   108
   156
2. 142.6
   100.75
   −72.85
   −80.6
3. −7.14
   −5.44
   1.26
   2.99
4. No   **5.** Yes   **6.** Yes   **7.** Yes   **8.** Yes
9. Yes   **10.** No   **11.** Yes   **12.** Yes   **13.** Yes
14. No   **15.** Yes   **16.** Yes   **17.** No   **18.** Yes
19. Yes   **20.** Yes   **21.** Yes   **22.** Yes
23. The graph is a circle of radius 5 with center at (0, 0).

CALCULATOR 19

1. (−2, 3)   **2.** (5, 4)   **3.** (17, 26)   **4.** (8.5, 6.4)
5. $z = 13$ **6.** $A = 3, B = 4$

CALCULATOR 20

1. 20.6 minutes   **2.** 0.5 hours   **3.** 4.2 ohms
4. 2.7 ohms   **5.** 19.9 ohms

CALCULATOR 21

1. 5   **2.** 13   **3.** −17.4   **4.** −1.09   **5.** 2.7×10^{21}
6. 10^8 or 100,000,000
7. 121, 144, 169, 196, 225, 256, 289, 324, 361, 400
8. 6   **9.** either 4 or 6   **10.** 120,409   **11.** 26; 34
12. No   **13.** 38   **14.** 85   **15.** 85   **16.** 937
17. 0.000000266

CALCULATOR 22

1. 103.146   **2.** 3.220   **3.** 80.137   **4.** 175.898
5. Error. Negative numbers do not have real square roots.
6. Both answers are the same. One expression is in the form $\sqrt{x^2 + 2xy + y^2}$ and the other is in the form $\sqrt{(x + y)^2}$ for $x = 17.4$ and $y = 2.7$. Thus the answer is $x + y$, or 20.1
7. 7   **8.** 13   **9.** 4   **10.** $x^{1/2} = \sqrt{x}$ **11.** $x^{1/2}$
12. $y^{-1/2}$ **13.** 5   **14.** 8   **15.** 11   **16.** 8   **17.** 12
18. 7   **19.** 4; $\sqrt[3]{8^2}$

CALCULATOR 23

1. 5   **2.** 100   **3.** 4   **4.** 7   **5.** 1.122462048   **6.** 5
7. 343   **8.** 128   **9.** 27   **10.** 16,807   **11.** 225
12. 32,768   **13.**   1
                 121
                12321
               1234321
14. 1234567654321   **15.** 3   **16.** 3   **17.** 63
18. 2   **19.** 24

CALCULATOR 24

1. 17-yes   **2.** 35-yes   **3.** 28-yes   **4.** 33.47-no
5. 94.89-no   **6.** 870-yes   **7.** 3, 4, 5   **8.** 33, 56, 65
9. 120, 442, 458   **10.** 285, 1612, 1637

CALCULATOR 25

1. −1544.199   **2.** 55.883, 0.619, 142.433
3. 0.142, 4.022, −0.262   **4.** 470.4   **5.** 470.4
6. −33,226.752   **7.** −1038.336   **8.** −4869.228
9. −993.72   **10.** Yes, no, no

CALCULATOR 26

1. (−3, −21)   **2.** (0.8, 2.8)   **3.** (−0.035, 19.088)
4. (0.3, −5.34)   **5.** (1, 19.6)   **6.** (−10.913, −179.451)
7. 0   **8.** ±2.3
9. Must solve $x = \sqrt{-12.88}$, which is undefined.
10. It does not.   **11.** Two, two   **12.** None, none

CALCULATOR 27

1.   56.4
    −55.46
2.   32.2
    −94.5
3. 61°F   **4.** 72°F   **5.** 48°F   **6.** 100°F   **7.** 40°F

CALCULATOR 28

1. 1.16 and −5.16   **2.** −2.06 and 0.56   **3.** −28; 0
4. 0; 1   **5.** 18   **6.** 53   **7.** 18   **8.** 11   **9.** −5
10. $18x^2 + 11x - 5 = 0$

CALCULATOR 29

1. 0.707   **2.** 0.532   **3.** −0.866   **4.** 0.007   **5.** 1
6. 0.796   **7.** Larger
8. 5.67
    57.29
    572.96
    57295.78
    57295779.51
9. Error; At 90° the adjacent side has length 0. Tan 90 = $\frac{\text{opposite}}{0}$, and we cannot divide by 0.
10. 0.676   **11.** 7.376   **12.** 0.694

CALCULATOR 30

1. 47°   **2.** 6°   **3.** 81°   **4.** 85°   **5.** 53°   **6.** 16°
7. 22°   68°   90°   **8.** 40°   50°   90°   **9.** 3°   87°   90°
10. 61°   29°   90°   **11.** 90°
12. 0.4067   0.6293   0.7660   **13.** 0.9135   0.7771   0.6428
14. 0.4452   0.8098   1.1918   **15.** 0.4452   0.8098   1.1918
16. the tangent of the angle.

CALCULATOR 31

1. 26.8 m   **2.** 5.2 km   **3.** 2243.1 mm   **4.** 36.9°
5. 46.8°   **6.** 51.1°   **7.** 77.9 ft   **8.** 19.0 yd   **9.** 11.5°

CALCULATOR 32

1. 301.88 ft   **2.** 316.67 ft   **3.** the 19th   **4.** 38.5
5. 0.69   **6.** 0.29   **7.** 2.17

Spreadsheet Activity Answers

SPREADSHEET ACTIVITY 1

1. Yes: for example, Ramos and Young. Extra-base hits contribute more than singles to slugging average, while each contributes the same to batting average.
2. 4 ways; (1B, 2B, 3B, HR): (6, 1, 0, 1), (6, 0, 2, 0), (5, 2, 1, 0), (4, 4, 0, 0)

3.

	A	B	C	D
1	Name	IP	ER	ERA
2	King	20	10	9*C2/B2

4. Garcia has the better average against both left-and right-handers, but Lutz has the better overall average.

Name	L	R	O
Garcia	.233	.378	.267
Lutz	.186	.329	.281

SPREADSHEET ACTIVITY 2

1. **a.** .5 **b.** .375 **c.** .714285714285... or $.\overline{714285}$
   d. .216666... or $.21\overline{6}$ **e.** .006 **f.** .634
   The fraction will convert to a terminating decimal if the denominator of the fraction is a power of 2 and/or 5. (Specifically, the denominator has the form 2^a5^b, where a and b are integer exponents.)
2. **a.** .5 **b.** .375 **c.** .006 **d.** .35 **e.** .38
   f. .0115 **g.** .734375
   The length of the decimal expansion is the power of 2 or 5, whichever is greater. (Specifically, the maximum of a and b from Exercise 1 is the length of the decimal expansion.)
3. **a.** $.\overline{3}$ **b.** $.\overline{142857}$ **c.** $.\overline{003}$
   d. $.\overline{63}$ **e.** $.3\overline{18}$
   f. $.2\overline{285714}$ **g.** $.0\overline{571428}$

4.

	A	B
1	1	
2	1	+A2/A1
3	+A1+A2	+A3/A2
4	+A2+A3	+A4/A3

The ratios eventually approach 1.618033..., the golden mean.

SPREADSHEET ACTIVITY 3

1. **a.** $-42 + 23x - 5x^2 - 12x^3 + 37x^4 + 15x^5$
   b. $8 - 16x + 8x^2 + x^3 + 3x^4 - 9x^5 + 5x^6$
2. **a.** $1 + 8x + 24x^2 + 32x^3 + 16x^4$
   b. $9 + 6x + 7x^2 + 2x^3 + x^4$
   c. $1 + 2x + 5x^2 + 4x^3 + 4x^4$
3. **a.** $-1 + x^4$
   b. $1 + 7x + 2x^2 + 10x^3 + 26x^4 + 3x^5 + 4x^6 + 12x^7$

4.

	A	B	C
2	5	7	8
3	2	1	6
5	+A2+A3	+B2+B3	+C2+C3

5.

	A	B	C
2	5	7	8
3	2	1	6
5	+A2−A3	+B2−B3	+C2−C3

SPREADSHEET ACTIVITY 4

1. Enter 32, 0 in B2, C2, and 212, 100 in B3, C3.
   98.6F = 37C; −40F = −40C.
2. $B = 0.15A + 25$, 130
3. **a.** $y = -2600x + 24000$, x = number of years from present.
   b. $11,000 **c.** 9.23 years from now. **d.** $63,000
4. **a.** $y = -2x + 15$, $y = 0.5x + 5$
   b. $y = -2x + 1$, $y = 0.5x + 6$
   c. $y = -2x + 2$, $y = 0.5x - 5.5$

SPREADSHEET ACTIVITY 5

1. 100 t-shirts; 300 t-shirts
2. 150 t-shirts, 300 t-shirts, 75 t-shirts
3. 150 t-shirts, 300 t-shirts 75 t-shirts
4. 5 Breakeven x = (C3 − B3)/(B2 − C2)
5. 133.3 or 134 t-shirts; 166.7 or 167 t-shirts; 200 t-shirts
6. **a.** 125 jackets **b.** 2000 jackets
7. **a.** 40 miles **b.** Alpha **c.** more than 40 miles
8. **a.** 5 min **b.** Data Access Corp
9. **a.** 20,000 bills **b.** less than 20,000 bills
   c. The cost would be equal at 12,000 bills.

SPREADSHEET ACTIVITY 6

1. 62 years after 1988 or in the year 2050; 86 years after 1988 or in the year 2074
2. With 1988 as year 0,

Country	India	China	Indonesia	Kenya
Year to Double	34	54	34	18
Pop in 2020	1556	1928	340	76

3.

Per Cent	1	2	3	4	5	6	7	8	9	10	11	12
Yrs (approx)	70	35	24	18	14	12	10	9	8	7	6.5	6

Years to Double $\approx$ 70/Rate
4. Answers will vary.

SPREADSHEET ACTIVITY 7

1. Mary. If her time is 5 days, the overall time is 3.158 days.
2. 10.286 hours 3. 12.436 or approximately $12\frac{1}{2}$ hours
4. When the slow train has a rate of 60 mph, the fast one has a rate of 80 mph, and the times will be equal.
5. 30 km/h, 70km/h

SPREADSHEET ACTIVITY 8

1. The positive estimates give 5.19615. The negative estimates give −5.19615.
2. The square root of a negative number is undefined. The procedure gives either ERROR or wild fluctuations. The cube root of a negative number is negative.
3. If x is an estimate of $\sqrt[4]{N}$, then $(3x + N/x^3)/4$ is a more accurate estimate of $\sqrt[4]{N}$.
   If x is an estimate of $\sqrt[5]{N}$, then $(4x + N/x^4)/5$ is a more accurate estimate of $\sqrt[5]{N}$.
   If x is an estimate of $\sqrt[n]{N}$, then $((n - 1)x + N/x^{n-1})/n$ is a more accurate estimate of $\sqrt[n]{N}$.
   a. 3, 3.16228, 3.76060, 4.16179
   b. 6, 6.17801, 3.98107, 3.12913

4.

	A	B
1	n	n!
2	1	1
3	1+A2	+A3*B2
4	1+A3	+A4*B3

SPREADSHEET ACTIVITY 9

1. **a.** 9.0, acute **b.** 7.63, right **c.** 8.71, obtuse

2. **a.**

	A	B	C
1	S1	S2	Hyp
2	5	12	@SQRT(A2^2+(B2^2))

b.

	A	B	C
1	Hyp	S1	S2
2	13	5	@SQRT(A2^2−(B2^2))

c. 13, 481, 172.0465 **d.** 220, 15.19868, 3.4641016
3. Answers will vary. Once a Pythagorean triple has been found, all multiples of that triple are Pythagorean triples.

SPREADSHEET ACTIVITY 10

1. Positive, 0, Negative

2.

Initial Height	0	100	200
Time of max ht	4.6875	4.6875	4.6875
Max Height	351.6	451.6	551.6
Time to ground	9.375	10	10.559
Impact Velocity	−150	−170	−188

3.

Initial Velocity	0	75	150	300
Time of max ht	0	2.344	4.688	9.375
Max Height	0	87.89	351.6	1406
Time to ground	0	4.688	9.375	18.75
Impact Velocity	0	−75	−150	−300

4.

Time	5.9	8.8	9.5	1.8
Impact Velocity	−188.5	−282.8	−305.1	−56.6

SPREADSHEET ACTIVITY 11

1. 1792.8 ft, 23.9%   **2.** 2.43 km   **3.** 188.1 m

4. a. approximately 982 ft   **b.** approx. 1180 ft
  c. 933.6 ft; Maria's

5. Replace D2 with the formula +A2*@SIN(C2) if the spreadsheet has trigonometric functions. Replace D2 with the formula +A2*(+C2−((C2^3)/6)+((C2^5)/120)−((C2^7)/5040)+((C2^9)/362880)) if your spreadsheet does not have trigonometric functions. The height is approx. 173 ft.

SPREADSHEET ACTIVITY 12

1. a. 86.28571   **b.** 84.25
2. a. 41.11428   **b.** 7.3283052   **3.** 94
4. a. 97 or higher   **b.** 95 or higher

BASIC COMPUTER PROJECT 1

EXERCISES

1. 40   PRINT 9*2*(5^2)

```
RUN
A = 2 B = 5
9A(B)^2 =
450
```
2. 40   PRINT (8+3*10)/5

```
RUN
A = 8 B = 10
(A + 3*B)/5 =
7.6
```

ON YOUR OWN

1.
```
10   REM EVALUATE EXPRESSIONS
20   PRINT ``10 + 3 × 5 = '';
30   PRINT 10 + (3*5)
40   PRINT ``(9 - 3)^2 = '';
50   PRINT (9 - 3)^2
60   PRINT ``9 - (3)^2 = '';
70   PRINT 9 - 3^2
80   END

RUN
10 + 3 × 5 = 25
(9 - 3)^2 = 36
9 - 3^2 = 0
```
2.
```
10   REM EVALUATE EXPRESSIONS 2
20   PRINT ``4 + 124 × 182 - 18='' 
25   PRINT 4 + 124*182 - 18
30   PRINT ``32 + 48 × 13/42 = '' 
35   PRINT 32 + 48 × 13/42
40   PRINT ``12 - 9/2 × 6 = '' 
45   PRINT 12 - 9/2 × 6
50   END

RUN
4 + 124 × 182 - 18 =
22554
32 + 48 × 13/42 =
800
12 - 9/2 × 6 =
7.50
```

3.
```
10   REM EVALUATE EXPRESSIONS 3
20   PRINT ``X = 7 Y = 3''
30   PRINT ``3X/(2Y + 1) = ''
40   PRINT 3*7/(2*3 + 1)
50   END

RUN
X = 7 Y = 3
3X/(2Y + 1) = 3
```
4.
```
10   REM EVALUATE EXPRESSIONS 4
20   PRINT ``C = 82''
30   PRINT ``C + 7/5*C^2 = ''
40   PRINT 82 + 7/5*8^2
50   END

RUN
C = 82
C + 7/5*C^2 =
171.6
```
5.
```
10   REM EVALUATE EXPRESSIONS 5
20   PRINT ``LET A = 4
30   PRINT ``7*A^6 = ''
40   PRINT 7*4^6
50   PRINT ``(7*A)^6 = ''
60   PRINT (7*4)^6
70   END

RUN
LET A = 4
7*A^6 =
28672
(7*A)^6 =
481890305
```
6.
```
10   REM EVALUATE EXPRESSIONS 6
20   PRINT ``WHEN B = 7, '';
30   PRINT ``9*(18*B + 8) = '';
40   PRINT 9*(18*7 + 8)
50   PRINT ``WHEN B = 20, '';
60   PRINT ``9*(18*B + 8) = '';
70   PRINT 9*(18*20 + 8)
80   PRINT ``WHEN B = 412, '';
90   PRINT ``9*(18*B + 8) = '';
100  PRINT 9*(18*412 + 8)

RUN
WHEN B = 7, 9*(18*B + 8) = 1206
WHEN B = 20, 9*(18*B + 8) = 3312
WHEN B = 412, 9*(18*B + 8) = 66816
```

BASIC COMPUTER PROJECT 2

EXERCISES

1. 3H = 2
  *B = 8
2. The value of W is 4

ON YOUR OWN

1.
```
10   REM FINDING SQUARES AND CUBES
20   LET X = -5.4
30   PRINT X*X
40   PRINT X*X*X
50   END

RUN
29.16
-157.464
```
2.
```
10   REM CIRCUMFERENCE AND AREA
20   LET R = 3.4
30   LET P = 3.14159
40   LET A = P*(R^2)
50   PRINT ``THE AREA IS''; A
60   LET C = 2*P*R
70   PRINT ``THE CIRCUMFERENCE IS''; C
80   END

RUN
THE AREA IS 36.3167805
THE CIRCUMFERENCE IS 21.362812
```

3.
```
10   REM VOLUME
20   LET B = 20
30   LET H = 6
40   LET V = B*H
50   PRINT ``THE VOLUME IS''; V; ``CM
     CUBED''
60   END

RUN
THE VOLUME IS 120 CM CUBED
```

4.
```
10   REM INTEREST
20   LET P = 4500
30   LET R = 0.114
40   LET T = 1
50   LET I = P*R*T
60   LET A = P + I
70   PRINT ``THE TOTAL DUE IS''; A
80   END

RUN
THE TOTAL DUE IS 5013
```

5.
```
10   LET A = 54.99
20   LET B = 26.75
30   LET C = 127.99
40   LET T = A + B + C
50   LET S = T*.07
60   LET D = S + T
70   PRINT ``THE TOTAL DUE IS''; D
80   END

RUN
THE TOTAL DUE IS 224.4111
```

6. Answers will vary.
```
5    REM EXAMPLE
10   LET AL = 1.2
20   LET DAN = 1.5
30   LET PETE = 2.5
40   LET JOHN = 2.1
50   LET BEN = 1.7
60   LET HEIGHT = AL + DAN + PETE + JOHN + BEN
70   LET AV = HEIGHT/5
80   PRINT ``AVERAGE HEIGHT = ''; AV; ``M''

RUN
AVERAGE HEIGHT = 1.8 M
```

BASIC COMPUTER PROJECT 3

EXERCISES

1. `40   PRINT MID$ (H$, 3, 3)`
2. `40   LET E$ = X$ + C$`

ON YOUR OWN

1.
```
10   LET A$ = ``A''
20   LET B$ = ``T''
30   LET C$ = ``R''
40   LET D$ = C$ + A$ + B$
50   LET E$ = B$ + A$ + C$
60   LET F$ = A$ + C$ + B$
70   PRINT D$, E$, F$

RUN
RAT TAR ART
```

2.
```
10   LET X$ = ``BULLETIN''
20   PRINT LEFT$ (X$,4)
30   PRINT MID$ (X$,4,3)
40   PRINT MID$ (X$,6,3)
50   PRINT MID$ (X$,7,2)

RUN
BULL
LET
TIN
IN
```

3.
```
10   LET S$ = ``DO YOU HAVE SIX CHAIRS?''
20   PRINT MID$ (S$,4,13) + MID$(S$,18,6)

RUN
YOU HAVE SIX HAIRS?
```

4.
```
10   LET A$ = ``JOHNSMITH''
20   PRINT LEFT$(A$,4)
30   PRINT MID$ (A$,5,5)

RUN
JOHN
SMITH
```

5.
```
10   LET A$ = ``RE''
20   LET B$ = ``PEAT''
30   LET C$ = ``VISE''
40   LET D$ = ``PEAL''
50   LET E$ = ``VIEW''
60   LET F$ = ``AP''
70   PRINT A$ + B$
80   PRINT A$ + C$
90   PRINT A$ + D$
100  PRINT A$ + E$
110  PRINT A$ + F$

RUN
REPEAT
REVISE
REPEAL
REVIEW
REAP
```

6.
```
10   REM EXAMPLE
20   LET A$ = ``2,4,5,1,3,5,7''
30   PRINT ``EVEN NUMBERS:''; LEFT$(A$,5)
50   PRINT ``ODD NUMBERS:''; MID$(A$,7,7)

RUN
EVEN NUMBERS: 2,4,6
ODD NUMBERS: 1,3,5,7
```

BASIC COMPUTER PROJECT 4

EXERCISES

1. A colon :
2. A comma ,

ON YOUR OWN

1.
```
10   REM POWERS
20   LET X = 23: Y = 34: Z = 48
25   X = 23
30   PRINT ``NUMBER'',
     ``SQUARE'',``CUBE''
40   PRINT X ,X^2,X^3
50   PRINT Y ,Y^2,Y^3
60   PRINT Z ,Z^2,Z^3
70   END

RUN
```
NUMBER	SQUARE	CUBE
23	529	12167
34	1156	39304
48	2304	110592

2.
```
10   LET T = 4130
20   LET I = .18
30   LET L = T*I
40   LET O = T–L
50   PRINT ``THE ORIGINAL LOAN WAS''; O

RUN
THE ORIGINAL LOAN WAS 3386.6
```

3.
```
10   LET A = 76: LET B = 89
20   LET Z = 88*3
30   LET S = Z – (A + B)
40   PRINT ``THE THIRD TEST WAS''; S

RUN
THE THIRD TEST WAS 99
```

```
4. 10   LET P = 3.1412: LET A = 16
   20   LET B = 8: LET D = 14
   30   LET C1 = P*A
   40   LET C2 = P*B
   50   LET C3 = P*D
   60   PRINT ``DIAMETER'',
        ``CIRCUMFERENCE''
   65   PRINT A,C1
   70   PRINT B,C2
   75   PRINT D,C3

   RUN
   DIAMETER   CIRCUMFERENCE
   16          50.2592
   8           25.1296
   14          43.9768
5. 10   REM PERIMETER
   20   LET A = 17: LET B = 23: LET C = 19:
        LET D = 11
   30   LET P = A + B + C + D
   40   PRINT P
   50   END

   RUN
   70
6. 5    REM PERCENTS
   10   LET A = 200: LET S = 450: LET D = 500:
        LET F = 700
   20   LET Q = 1.75*A: PRINT Q
   30   LET W = 1.75*S: PRINT W
   40   LET E = 1.75*D: PRINT E
   50   LET R = 1.75*F: PRINT R
   60   END

   RUN
   350
   787.5
   875
   1225
```

BASIC COMPUTER PROJECT 5

EXERCISES

```
1. 40   INPUT Y,A
2. 20   INPUT N$,A,B
```

ON YOUR OWN

```
1. 10   PRINT ``INPUT A TEMPERATURE IN
        CELSIUS''
   20   INPUT C
   30   LET F = (9/5*C) + 32
   40   PRINT F

   RUN
   INPUT A TEMPERATURE IN CELSIUS
   ?10
   50
2. 10   PRINT ``ENTER 5 SCORES, SEPARATED BY A
        COMMA''
   20   INPUT A,B,C,D,E
   30   LET Z = (A + B + C + D + E)/5
   40   PRINT ``THE AVERAGE SCORE IS '';Z

   RUN
   ENTER 5 SCORES, SEPARATED BY A COMMA
   ?90,80,70,60,50
   THE AVERAGE SCORE IS 70
```

```
3. 10   PRINT ``TYPE THE LENGTH OF THE
        RECTANGLE''
   20   INPUT L: PRINT
   30   PRINT ``TYPE THE WIDTH OF THE
        RECTANGLE''
   40   INPUT W
   50   LET P = (2*L) + (2*W)
   60   PRINT ``THE PERIMETER IS '';P
   70   LET A = L*W
   80   PRINT ``THE AREA IS '';A

   RUN
   TYPE THE LENGTH OF THE RECTANGLE
   ?3
   TYPE THE WIDTH OF THE RECTANGLE
   ?2
   THE PERIMETER IS 10
   THE AREA IS 6
4. 10   PRINT ``TYPE YOUR NAME''
   20   INPUT N$
   30   PRINT ``HOW MANY KM TRAVELED?''
   40   INPUT D
   50   PRINT ``RATE OF SPEED?''
   60   INPUT R
   70   LET T = D/R
   80   PRINT ``YOUR TRIP TOOK '';T;
        ``HOURS,'';N$

   RUN
   TYPE YOUR NAME
   ?MARYANN
   HOW MANY KM TRAVELED?
   ?100
   RATE OF SPEED?
   ?50
   YOUR TRIP TOOK 2 HOURS, MARYANN
5. 10   PRINT ``TYPE AN EVEN INTEGER''
   20   INPUT I
   30   LET C = I + (I + 2)
   40   PRINT I,I + 2,C

   RUN
   TYPE AN EVEN INTEGER
   ?10
   10     12     22
6. 10   PRINT ``INPUT BASE OF TRIANGLE''
   20   INPUT B
   30   PRINT ``INPUT HEIGHT OF TRIANGLE''
   40   INPUT H
   50   LET A = (B*H)/2
   60   PRINT ``THE AREA OF THE TRIANGLE IS '';
        A
   70   LET X = 3*B: LET Y = 3*H
   80   LET R = (X*Y)/2
   90   PRINT ``THE AREA OF THOSE MEASURES ×3
        IS '';R

   RUN
   INPUT BASE OF TRIANGLE
   ?10
   INPUT HEIGHT OF TRIANGLE
   ?5
   THE AREA OF THE TRIANGLE IS 25
   THE AREA OF THOSE MEASURES ×3 IS 225
```

BASIC COMPUTER PROJECT 6

EXERCISES
1. 30   HTAB 16: VTAB 12
2. 60   HOME: VTAB 12: HTAB 12

ON YOUR OWN
1. 10   LET A = 3:B = 5:C = 10
   20   HOME
   30   PRINT``(A + B)^2 + C = ``; (A + B)^2 + C
   40   PRINT ``PRESS RETURN``: INPUT R$
   50   HOME
   60   PRINT ``(A×B)^2*(A×C)^2 = ``;
        (A*B)^2*(A*C)^2

   RUN
   (A + B)^2 + C = 74
   PRESS RETURN
   ?
   (A×B)^2*(A×C)^2 = 202500
2. 10   PRINT ``TYPE YOUR LAST NAME``
   20   INPUT L$
   30   PRINT: PRINT ``TYPE YOUR FIRST NAME``
   40   INPUT F$: PRINT
   50   PRINT ``TYPE YOUR MIDDLE INITIAL``
   60   INPUT M$
   70   HOME: VTAB 12: HTAB 12
   80   PRINT F$;`` ``; M$;`` ``; L$

   RUN
   TYPE YOUR LAST NAME
   ?BLOCK
   TYPE YOUR FIRST NAME
   ?MARYANN
   TYPE YOUR MIDDLE INITIAL
   ?K
   MARYANN K BLOCK
3. 10   LET P = 197
   20   LET T = .06
   30   LET S = P*T
   50   HOME : VTAB 10
   60   PRINT ``THE SALES TAX IS``; S
   70   PRINT : PRINT ``THE TOTAL COST IS ``;
        P + S

   RUN
   THE SALES TAX IS 11.82
   THE TOTAL COST IS 208.82
4. 10   PRINT ``TYPE THE LENGTH OF THE SIDE OF
        A SQUARE``
   20   INPUT L
   30   P = 4*L
   40   PRINT ``THE PERIMETER IS``; P
   50   PRINT ``PRESS RETURN``
   60   INPUT R$
   70   LET A = L*L
   80   HOME
   90   PRINT ``THE AREA OF THE SQUARE IS ``; A

   RUN
   TYPE THE LENGTH OF THE SIDE OF A SQUARE
   ?5
   THE PERIMETER IS 20
   PRESS RETURN
   ?
   THE AREA OF THE SQUARE IS 25

BASIC COMPUTER PROJECT 7

EXERCISES
1. 60   PRINT N$, X, Y
2. 20   READ A, B, C, D

ON YOUR OWN
1. 10   READ C
   20   READ (3*C)^2 + (9*C) - 4
   30   GOTO 10
   40   DATA -5, 3, .2, 5.5

   RUN
   176
   104
   -1.84
   317.75
2. 10   PRINT ``THE SOLUTIONS ARE``
   20   READ P
   30   LET Q = (P + 5) - 7
   40   PRINT ``(``P; ``,``Q``)``
   50   GOTO 20
   60   DATA -3, .4, 11, 5.2, -.6

   RUN
   THE SOLUTIONS ARE
   (-3, -5)
   (.4, -1.6)
   (11, 9)
   (5.2, 3.2)
   (-.6, -2.6)
3. 10   PRINT ``THE AREAS ARE:``
   20   READ B, H
   30   PRINT (B*H)/2
   40   GOTO 20
   50   DATA 7, 8.4, 9.3, .9, 18.2, 23, 6.4, 3.8

   RUN
   THE AREAS ARE:
   29.4
   4.185
   209.3
   12.16
4. 10   PRINT ``X``,``Y``,``Z``
   20   READ X, Y
   30   Z = 5*(X^2) + (3*X*Y) - (Y^2)
   40   PRINT X, Y, Z
   50   GOTO 20
   60   DATA .2, .5, 2, 5, -2, -5, 2.2, 5.5

   RUN
   X   Y   Z
   .2   .5   .25
   2   5   25
   -2   -5   25
   2.2   5.5   30.25
5. 10   READ N$ A, B, C
   20   LET V = (A + B + C)/3
   30   PRINT N$, V
   40   GOTO 10
   50   DATA MARIA, 96, 94, 98, JEFF, 92, 89, 93
   60   DATA SARA, 75, 85, 95, JASON, 83, 68, 72

   RUN
   MARIA   96
   JEFF   91.3333334
   SARA   85
   JASON   74.3333334

6.
```
10 HTAB 15 : PRINT ``POWERS''
20 PRINT ``FOURTH'',``FIFTH'',``SIXTH''
30 READ A
40 PRINT A^4,A^5,A^6
50 GOTO 30
60 DATA -2, .4, 5, 10, -.3, 7

RUN
                    POWERS
FOURTH              FIFTH           SIXTH
16                  -32             64
.0256000001         .01024          4.09600001E-03
625                 3125            15625
10000               100000          1000000
8.10000001E-03      -2.43E-03       7.29000001E-04
2401                16807           117649
```

BASIC COMPUTER PROJECT 8

EXERCISES

1. `20 IF A<B THEN GOTO 50`

2. `30 IF Z = -2.45 + 45 THEN GOTO 60`

ON YOUR OWN

1.
```
10 PRINT ``TYPE ANY NUMBER''
20 INPUT X
30 IF X>0 THEN GOTO 60
40 IF X<0 THEN GOTO 70
50 PRINT ``YOUR NUMBER IS 0''
55 GOTO 90
60 PRINT ``YOUR NUMBER IS POSITIVE''
65 GOTO 90
70 PRINT ``YOUR NUMBER IS NEGATIVE''
90 END

RUN
TYPE ANY NUMBER
?3
YOUR NUMBER IS POSITIVE
```

2.
```
10 READ A
20 LET P = 0.5*(A + 5)
30 LET Q = 0.2*(3 + A)
40 IF P<Q THEN PRINT A;`` IS A SOLUTION''
50 IF P>Q THEN PRINT A;`` IS NOT A
   SOLUTION''
60 GOTO 10
70 DATA -100, -30, -9, -6.5, -6.3, -6, -5.5, 0

RUN
-100 IS A SOLUTION
-30 IS A SOLUTION
-9 IS A SOLUTION
-6.5 IS A SOLUTION
-6.3 IS NOT A SOLUTION
-6 IS NOT A SOLUTION
-5.5 IS NOT A SOLUTION
0 IS NOT A SOLUTION
```

3.
```
10 PRINT ``TYPE TWO NUMBERS, ONE AT A
   TIME''
20 INPUT A,S
30 PRINT ``DO YOU WANT THEIR SUM OR
   PRODUCT?''
40 INPUT R$
50 IF R$ = ``SUM'' THEN GOTO 80
60 PRINT ``THE PRODUCT OF ''; A ;
   `` AND ''; S; `` IS ''; A*S
70 GOTO 90
80 PRINT ``THE SUM OF ''; A; `` AND''; S;
   `` IS ''; A + S
90 END

RUN
TYPE TWO NUMBERS, ONE AT A TIME
?2
??5
DO YOU WANT THEIR SUM OR PRODUCT?
?SUM
THE SUM OF 2 AND 5 IS 7
```

4.
```
10 PRINT ``TYPE 5 SCORES, SEPARATED BY
   COMMAS''
20 INPUT A, B, C, D, E
30 LET Z = (A + B + C + D + E)/5
40 IF Z<75 THEN GOTO 70
50 PRINT ``YOU RECEIVED A PASSING GRADE''
70 END

RUN
TYPE 5 SCORES, SEPARATED BY COMMAS
?60, 90, 100, 100, 90
YOU RECEIVED A PASSING GRADE
```

5.
```
10 PRINT ``TYPE ANY POSITIVE OR NEGATIVE
   NUMBER''
20 INPUT N
30 IF N<0 THEN GOTO 60
40 PRINT ``YOUR NUMBER IS POSITIVE''
50 GOTO 90
60 PRINT ``YOUR NUMBER IS NEGATIVE''
70 PRINT ``ITS ABSOLUTE VALUE IS''; -(N)
90 END

RUN
TYPE ANY POSITIVE OR NEGATIVE NUMBER
?4
YOUR NUMBER IS POSITIVE
```

6.
```
10 REM COMPUTER PROJECT
20 PRINT ``(X + 1)(X - 1)'',``(X^2 - 1)''
30 READ X
40 LET Q = (X + 1)*(X - 1)
50 LET P = X^2 - 1
60 PRINT Q, P
70 GOTO 30
80 DATA 2, 20, 37.5, 40, 47, 2134
90 END

RUN
(X + 1)(X - 1)    (X^2 - 1)
3                 3
399               399
1405.25           1405.25
1599              1599
2208              2208
4553955           4553955
```

BASIC COMPUTER PROJECT 9

EXERCISES

1. `30 PRINT ABS(A + B)`

2. 90

ON YOUR OWN

1.
```
10 FOR X = 1 TO 10
20 LET Y = SQR(X)
40 PRINT X,Y
70 NEXT X

RUN
1    1
2    1.41421356
3    1.73205081
4    2
5    2.23606798
6    2.44948974
7    2.64575131
8    2.82842713
9    3
10   3.16227766
```

```
2. 10    LET Z = INT(25*RND(1)) + 1
   20    PRINT ``GUESS MY NUMBER''
   30    INPUT A
   40    IF A>Z THEN GOTO 70
   50    IF A<Z THEN GOTO 80
   60    PRINT ``THAT'S IT!''
   65    GOTO 100
   70    PRINT ``YOUR GUESS IS TOO HIGH''
   75    GOTO 90
   80    PRINT ``YOUR GUESS IS TOO LOW''
   90    GOTO 20
   100   END

   RUN
   GUESS MY NUMBER
   ?2
   YOUR GUESS IS TOO LOW
3. 10    PRINT ``TYPE TWO NEGATIVE NUMBERS''
   20    INPUT A,B
   30    PRINT ``THE ABSOLUTE VALUE OF THE
         DIFFERENCE''
   40    PRINT ``BETWEEN THESE NUMBERS IS'';
         ABS(A-B)

   RUN
   TYPE TWO NEGATIVE NUMBERS
   ?-6,-7
   THE ABSOLUTE VALUE OF THE DIFFERENCE BETWEEN
   THESE NUMBERS IS 1
4. 10    FOR X = 25 TO 34
   20    LET Z = SQR(X)
   25    PRINT Z
   30    LET T = T + Z
   35    NEXT X
   40    PRINT ``THE SUM IS''; T

   RUN
   5
   5.09901951
   5.19615243
   5.29150263
   5.38516481
   5.47722558
   5.56776437
   5.65685425
   5.74456265
   5.8309519
   THE SUM IS 54.2491981
5. 10    PRINT ``TYPE A 3-DIGIT NUMBER''
   20    INPUT N
   30    FOR T = 1 TO SQR(N)
   40    LET Z = N/T
   50    IF Z<>INT(Z) THEN GOTO 80
   60    PRINT T; ``AND''; Z; ``ARE FACTORS''
   80    NEXT T

   RUN
   TYPE A 3-DIGIT NUMBER
   ?899
   1 AND 899 ARE FACTORS
   29 AND 31 ARE FACTORS
6. 10    PRINT ``INPUT ANY INTEGER''
   20    INPUT Z
   30    PRINT 100*SQR(Z)

   RUN
   INPUT ANY INTEGER
   ?5
   223.606798
```

BASIC COMPUTER PROJECT 10

EXERCISES

1. 10,8,6,4,2,0
2. 30   PRINT C,C^2,SQR(C)

ON YOUR OWN

```
1. 10    FOR X = 20 TO 30
   20    PRINT X,X*X,X*X*X
   30    NEXT X

   RUN
   20    400    8000
   21    441    9261
   22    484    10648
   23    529    12167
   24    576    13824
   25    625    15625
   26    676    17576
   27    729    19683
   28    784    21952
   29    841    24389
   30    900    27000
2. 10    LET Z = INT(25*RND(1)) + 1
   20    FOR X = 1 TO 3
   30    PRINT ``GUESS MY NUMBER''
   40    INPUT G
   50    IF G>Z THEN GOTO 80
   60    IF G<Z THEN GOTO 90
   70    PRINT ``THAT'S MY NUMBER!''
   75    GOTO 120
   80    PRINT ``YOUR GUESS IS TOO HIGH.''
   85    GOTO 100
   90    PRINT ``YOUR GUESS IS TOO LOW.''
   100   NEXT X
   110   PRINT ``MY NUMBER IS''; Z; ``.''
   120   END

   RUN
   GUESS MY NUMBER
   ?4
   YOUR GUESS IS TOO LOW.
   GUESS MY NUMBER
   ?7
   YOUR GUESS IS TOO LOW.
   GUESS MY NUMBER
   ?9
   YOUR GUESS IS TOO LOW.
   MY NUMBER IS 21
3. 10    FOR X = 1 TO 5
   20    READ F
   30    LET C = (5/9*F)-32
   40    PRINT F,C
   50    NEXT X
   60    DATA 100,32,98,50,25

   RUN
   100   23.5555556
   32    -14.2222222
   98    22.4444444
   50    -4.22222223
   25    -18.1111111
4. 5     PRINT ``AREA'', ``VOLUME''
   10    FOR X = 1 TO 5
   20    READ E
   30    LET A = 6*E^2
   40    LET V = E^3
   50    PRINT A,V
   60    NEXT X
   70    DATA 3,4.2,2,3,8,9.4
   80    END

   RUN
   AREA      VOLUME
   54        27
   105.84    74.088
   24        8
   54        27
   384       512
```

```
5. 10   FOR X = 2 TO 20 STEP 2
   20   PRINT X; `` + ''; X + 2; `` = ''; X + (X + 2)
   30   FOR T = 1 TO 50: NEXT T
   40   NEXT X

   RUN
   2  + 4  = 6
   4  + 6  = 10
   6  + 8  = 14
   8  + 10 = 18
   10 + 12 = 22
   12 + 14 = 26
   14 + 16 = 30
   16 + 18 = 34
   18 + 20 = 38
   20 + 22 = 42
6. 10   FOR X = 1 TO 10
   20   LET S = SQR(X)
   30   LET I = INT(S)
   40   LET T = T + 1
   50   NEXT X
   60   PRINT ``THE SUM OF THE INTEGER
        VALUES''
   70   PRINT ``OF THE SQUARE ROOTS OF 1 TO 10
        IS ''; T

   RUN
   THE SUM OF THE INTEGER VALUES
   OF THE SQUARE ROOTS OF 1 TO 10 IS 19
```

BASIC COMPUTER PROJECT 11

EXERCISES

1. 20,10
2. horizontal line, X, Y
3. vertical line, 25, 05
4. 10,3
5. 30   COLOR = 15
6. 30   LET C = INT(16*RND(1))

ON YOUR OWN

```
1. 10   GR : COLOR = 13
   20   FOR X = 0 TO 39
   30   FOR Y = 0 TO 39
   40   PLOT X,Y : NEXT Y,X
2. 10   GR : COLOR = 10
   20   FOR X = 0 TO 39
3. 10   GR
   20   FOR I = 1 TO 30
   30   COLOR = INT(RND(1)*16)
   40   HLIN 10,30 AT Y
   45   Y = Y + 1
   50   NEXT I
4. 5    GR
   10   FOR I = 1 TO 500
   20   X = INT(RND(1)*40)
   30   Y = INT(RND(1)*40)
   40   COLOR = INT(RND(1)*16)
   50   PLOT X,Y
   60   NEXT
```

BASIC COMPUTER PROJECT 12

EXERCISES

1. 60   COLOR = 0
2. 60   HLIN 5,10 AT Y

ON YOUR OWN

```
1. 10   GR
   20   FOR X = 0 TO 39
   30   COLOR = 10
   40   PLOT X,X
   45   FOR A = 1 TO 80 : NEXT
   50   COLOR = 0
   60   PLOT X,X
   70   NEXT
```

```
2. 10   GR
   20   FOR X = 39 TO 0 STEP -1
   30   COLOR = 10
   40   PLOT X,X
   45   FOR A = 1 TO 80: NEXT
   50   COLOR = 0
   60   PLOT X,X
   70   NEXT
3. 10   GR
   20   FOR Y = 0 TO 39
   30   COLOR = 9
   40   HLIN 0,39 AT Y
   50   FOR A = 1 TO 80 : NEXT
   60   COLOR = 0
   70   HLIN 0,39 AT Y
   80   NEXT
4. 10   GR
   20   FOR Y = 39 TO 0 STEP -1
   30   COLOR = 9
   40   VLIN 0,39 AT Y
   50   FOR A = 1 TO 80: NEXT
   60   COLOR = 0
   70   VLIN 0,39 AT Y
   80   NEXT
5. 10   GR
   20   FOR Y = 0 TO 39
   30   COLOR = 6
   40   PLOT 20,Y: PLOT 20,(39-Y)
   50   FOR A = 1 TO 80: NEXT
   60   COLOR = 0
   70   PLOT 20,Y: PLOT 20,(39-Y)
   80   NEXT
6. 10   GR
   20   FOR Y = 0 TO 39
   30   COLOR = 6
   40   HLIN 0,39 AT Y: HLIN 0,39 AT (39-Y)
   50   FOR A = 1 TO 80: NEXT
   60   COLOR = 0
   70   HLIN 0,39 AT Y: HLIN 0,39 AT (39-Y)
   80   NEXT
```

BASIC COMPUTER PROJECT 13

EXERCISES

1. 50, 10, 50
2. 20   HGR
3. a rectangle
4. 5

ON YOUR OWN

```
1. 5    HGR
   10   HCOLOR = 3
   15   HPLOT 0,105 TO 279,105
   20   HPLOT 140,0 TO 140,190
   25   FOR X = 1 TO 50
   30   Y = 2*X + 5
   40   HPLOT X + 140,105-Y
   50   NEXT
2. 20   HGR: HCOLOR = INT(RND(1)*7)
   30   FOR N = 1 TO 100
   40   X = INT(RND(1)*100)
   50   Y = INT(RND(1)*100)
   60   HPLOT X,Y
   70   NEXT
3. 10   HGR
   20   HCOLOR = 3
   30   FOR I = 1 TO 6
   40   READ L
   50   HPLOT 0,0 TO L,0 TO L,60 TO 0,60 TO 0,0
   60   FOR A = 1 TO 300: NEXT
   70   HGR2
   80   NEXT
   100  DATA 20,30,50,60,90,40
4. 10   HGR
   15   HCOLOR = 3
   20   READ L,D,F
   30   HPLOT F,F TO L,D TO F,D TO G,F
   40   DATA 100,150,0
```

BASIC COMPUTER PROJECT 14

EXERCISES

1. 10 PRINT ``X + Y = 16''
   20 PRINT ``X - Y = 2''

2. 30 PRINT ``2X = 18''

ON YOUR OWN

1. 10 X = 27/3
   20 PRINT ``ONE NUMBER IS: ''; X
   30 PRINT ``THE OTHER NUMBER IS: ''; 2*X-1

   RUN
   ONE NUMBER IS: 9
   THE OTHER NUMBER IS: 17

2. 10 PRINT ``X + Y = 25''
   20 PRINT ``X - Y = 5''
   30 LET X = 30/2
   40 Y = 25-X
   50 PRINT ``MARIA IS ''; Y; ``YEARS OLD''
   60 PRINT ``JEFF IS''; X; ``YEARS OLD''
   70 END

   RUN
   X + Y = 25
   X - Y = 5
   MARIA IS 10 YEARS OLD
   JEFF IS 15 YEARS OLD

3. 10 INPUT ``ENTER TWO NUMBERS ''; X,Y
   20 PRINT ``THEIR SUM IS: ''; X + Y
   30 PRINT ``THEIR DIFFERENCE IS: ''; X-Y

   RUN
   ENTER TWO NUMBERS 6,90
   THEIR SUM IS: 96
   THEIR DIFFERENCE IS: -84

4. 10 INPUT ``ENTER TWO AGES''; A,B
   20 X = A + B : Y = A-B
   30 PRINT ``TWO PEOPLE HAVE AGES WHOSE
       SUM IS''; X; ``, AND WHOSE DIFFERENCE
       IS''; Y; ``. FIND THEIR AGES.''

   RUN
   ENTER TWO AGES 50,30
   TWO PEOPLE HAVE AGES WHOSE SUM IS 80, AND
   WHOSE DIFFERENCE IS 20. FIND THEIR AGES

5. 10 X = (1.95-.2)/(.25 + .1)
   20 PRINT ``KELLY HAS''; X; `` QUARTERS
       AND''; X + 2; ``DIMES''

   RUN
   KELLY HAS 5 QUARTERS AND 7 DIMES

6. 10 INPUT ``NUMBER OF NICKELS?''; N
   20 INPUT ``NUMBER OF DIMES?''; D
   30 PRINT ``THE TOTAL AMOUNT IS: $'';
       .05*N + .1*D
   40 PRINT ``THE TOTAL AMOUNT OF COINS
       IS:''; N + D
   50 PRINT ``SOMEONE HAD''; D-N; ``MORE
       DIMES THAN NICKELS. THE TOTAL AMOUNT
       OF MONEY WAS$''; .05*N + .1*D
   60 PRINT ``FIND THE AMOUNT OF EACH COIN.''

   RUN
   NUMBER OF NICKELS? 7
   NUMBER OF DIMES? 9
   THE TOTAL AMOUNT IS: $1.25
   THE TOTAL AMOUNT OF COINS IS: 16
   SOMEONE HAD 2 MORE DIMES THAN NICKELS
   THE TOTAL AMOUNT OF MONEY WAS $1.25
   FIND THE AMOUNT OF EACH COIN.

BASIC COMPUTER PROJECT 15

EXERCISES

1. 10 PRINT ``THE HYPOTENUSE IS ''; 5*100;
       ``CM LONG.''

2. 10 X = (7 + 2*SQR(3))*(7 - 2*SQR(3))

ON YOUR OWN

1. 10 INPUT ``ENTER THE LENGTH OF ONE LEG'';
       A
   20 INPUT ``ENTER THE LENGTH OF THE OTHER
       LEG''; B
   30 C = SQR(A^2 + B^2)
   40 PRINT ``THE LENGTH OF THE HYPOTENUSE
       IS: ''; C

   RUN
   ENTER THE LENGTH OF ONE LEG 3
   ENTER THE LENGTH OF THE OTHER LEG 4
   THE LENGTH OF THE HYPOTENUSE IS: 5

2. 10 A = 3:B = 16:D = 34
   20 C = SQR(A^2 + B^2)
   25 IF D = C THEN 100
   30 PRINT ``IT IS NOT A RIGHT TRIANGLE''
   50 END
   100 PRINT ``YES, 34 IS THE HYPOTENUSE.''

   RUN
   IT IS NOT A RIGHT TRIANGLE

3. 10 B = 607.2:H = 7.2
   20 A = B/2*H
   30 PRINT ``THE AREA IS''; A; ``SQUARE
       CENTIMETERS''

   RUN
   THE AREA IS 2185.92 SQUARE CENTIMETERS

4. 10 B = 12:C = 96
   20 A = SQR(C^2 - B^2)
   30 PRINT ``THE LENGTH OF THE OTHER LEG IS
       ''; A; ``CM.''

   RUN
   THE LENGTH OF THE OTHER LEG IS
   95.2470473 CM.

5. 10 S = 90
   20 A = S^2:P = 4*S:L = SQR(2)*S
   30 PRINT ``AREA = ''; A
   40 PRINT ``PERIMETER = ''; P
   50 PRINT ``LENGTH OF THE DIAGONAL = ''; L

   RUN
   AREA = 8100
   PERIMETER = 360
   LENGTH OF THE DIAGONAL = 127.279221

6. 10 C = 34:B = 30
   20 A = SQR(C^2 - B^2)
   30 PRINT ``THE FOOT OF THE LADDER IS ''; A;
       `` FEET AWAY FROM THE BASE OF THE WALL.''

   RUN
   THE FOOT OF THE LADDER IS 16 FEET AWAY FROM
   THE BASE OF THE WALL.

BASIC COMPUTER PROJECT 16

EXERCISES

1. 10   DEF FN F(X) = ABS(X - 2)

2. 100   FOR X1 = 0 TO 279 STEP .2
(Note program will run very slowly.)

ON YOUR OWN

1.
```
10    DEF FN F(X) = ABS(X - 2)
15    DEF FN G(X) = ABS(X + 2)
20    X0 = 135:Y0 = 100
30    HGR2
40    REM **DRAW AXES**
50    HCOLOR = 3
60    HPLOT 0,Y0 TO 279,Y0
70    HPLOT X0,0 TO X0,191
80    REM **PLOT FUNCTION**
90    HCOLOR = 3
100   FOR X1 = 0 TO 279 STEP .5
110   X = (X1 - X0)/10
120   Y = FN F(X)
130   Y1 = Y0 - 10*Y
140   IF (Y1 > = 0) AND (Y1 < = 191) THEN HPLOT
      X1,Y1
150   NEXT X1
160   FOR X1 = 0 TO 279 STEP .5
170   X = (X1 - X0)/10
180   Y = FN G(X)
190   Y1 = Y0 - 10*Y
200   IF (Y1 > = 0) AND (Y1 < = 191) THEN HPLOT
      X1,Y1
210   NEXT X1
220   END
```

For 2-4, modify program 1 as follows. Note that these functions may take a minute or two before appearing on the screen.

2. 10   DEF FN F(X) = ABS(3*X - 2)
   15   DEF FN G(X) = ABS(-3*X - 2)
3. 10   DEF FN F(X) = X^2 + 3*X + 1
   15   DEF FN G(X) = X^2 - 3*X - 1
4. 10   DEF FN F(X) = X^3 + 2*X^2 - 5*X - 6
   15   DEF FN G(X) = -X^3 - 2*X^2 + 5*X + 6

BASIC COMPUTER PROJECT 17

EXERCISES

1. 30   IF (B^2) - (4*A*C) < 0 THEN 80

2. 50   S2 = (-B - SQR(B^2 - 4*A*C))/(2*A)

ON YOUR OWN

1.
```
10    READ A,B,C
20    X1 = ( -B + SQR(B^2 - 4*A*C))/(2*A)
30    X2 = ( -B - SQR(B^2 - 4*A*C))/(2*A)
40    PRINT ``THE ROOTS ARE: ''; X1; ``,'';
      X2
50    N = N + 1: IF N = 2 THEN END
60    GOTO 10
100   DATA 3,1, -1,1,2, -24

RUN
THE ROOTS ARE: .434258546, -.767591879
THE ROOTS ARE: 4, -6
```

2.
```
10    READ A,B,C
15    IF B^2 - 4*A*C < 0 THEN 50
20    X1 = ( -B + SQR(B^2 - 4*A*C))/(2*A)
30    X2 = ( -B - SQR(B^2 - 4*A*C))/(2*A)
40    PRINT ``THE ROOTS ARE: ''; X1; ``,'';
      X2
50    N = N + 1: IF N = 3 THEN END
60    GOTO 10
100   DATA 1, -8,15,3, -6,1,5,5, -1

RUN
THE ROOTS ARE: 5,3
THE ROOTS ARE: 1.81649658, .183503419
THE ROOTS ARE .170820394, -1.17082039
```

3.
```
10    READ A,B,C
15    IF B^2 - 4*A*C < 0 THEN 50
20    X1 = ( -B + SQR(B^2 - 4*A*C))/(2*A)
30    X2 = ( -B - SQR(B^2 - 4*A*C))/(2*A)
40    PRINT ``THE ROOTS ARE: ''; X1; ``,'';
      X2
50    N = N + 1: IF N = 2 THEN END
60    GOTO 10
100   DATA 9,0, -4,8,0, -3

RUN
THE ROOTS ARE: .666666667, -.666666667
THE ROOTS ARE: .612372436, -.612372436
```

4.
```
10    READ A,B,C
15    IF B^2 - 4*A*C < 0 THEN 120
20    X1 = ( -B + SQR(B^2 - 4*A*C))/(2*A)
30    X2 = ( -B - SQR(B^2 - 4*A*C))/(2*A)
40    PRINT ``THE ROOTS ARE: ''; X1; ``,'';
      X2
50    N = N + 1: IF N = 3 THEN END
60    GOTO 10
100   DATA 1,2, -2,2,1,3,3,0, -12
120   PRINT ``THE EQUATION ''A; ``X^2 + ''B;
      ``X + ''C; `` HAS NO REAL NUMBER
      SOLUTION.''

RUN
THE ROOTS ARE: .732050808, -2.73205081
THE EQUATION 2X^2 + 1X + 3 HAS NO REAL
NUMBER SOLUTION.
THE ROOTS ARE: 2, -2
```

5.
```
10    REM THE FORMULA IS B^2 + 18B - 180 = 0
20    A = 1:B = 18:C = -180
30    Y = ( -B + SQR(B^2 - 4*A*C))/(2*A)
40    PRINT ``ONE NUMBER IS: ''; Y; ``, AND
      THE OTHER IS: ''; Y + 18

RUN
ONE NUMBER IS: 7.15549443, AND THE OTHER IS:
25.1554944
LIST
```

6.
```
10    REM THE EQUATION IS B^2 - 6.5B - 12 = 0
20    A = 1:B = -6.5:C = -12
30    Y = ( -B + SQR(B^2 - 4*A*C))/(2*A)
40    PRINT ``THE LENGTH IS: ''; Y; `` THE
      WIDTH IS:''(11 - Y)/2

RUN
THE LENGTH IS:8      THE WIDTH IS:1.5
```

BASIC COMPUTER PROJECT 18

EXERCISES

1. 40   FOR P = 500 TO 650 STEP 50
   60   NEXT P
2. 10   READ R
  100   DATA .11,.13,.15,.17

ON YOUR OWN

1.
```
5     HOME
10    P = 750:R = .007*12:T = 24
20    A = P*(1 + R)^T
30    PRINT ``THE YIELD IS $''; A

RUN
THE YIELD IS $5197.13557
```

2.
```
5     FOR P = 800 TO 1400 STEP 100
10    R = .007*12:T = 24
20    A = P*(1 + R)^T
30    PRINT ``THE YIELD FOR $''; P; `` IS $'';
      A
40    NEXT P

RUN
THE YIELD FOR $800 IS $5543.61128
THE YIELD FOR $900 IS $6236.56268
THE YIELD FOR $1000 IS $6929.51409
THE YIELD FOR $1100 IS $7622.4655
THE YIELD FOR $1200 IS $8315.41692
THE YIELD FOR $1300 IS $9008.36832
THE YIELD FOR $1400 IS $9701.31973
```

94   *Algebra Technology*

```
3.  5   FOR I = 1 TO 3
   10   READ R
   20   P = 2000:T = 3
   30   A = P*(1 + R)^T
   40   PRINT ``THE YIELD AT '';R*100;``% IS
        $'';A
   50   NEXT I
   60   DATA .085,.0875,.129

   RUN
   THE YIELD AT 8.5% IS $2554.57825
   THE YIELD AT 8.75% IS $2572.27735
   THE YIELD AT 12.9% IS $2878.13938
4.  5   HOME
   10   A = 3763.20:R = .12:T = 2
   20   P = A/(1 + R)^T
   30   PRINT ``THE ORIGINAL IS $'';P

   RUN
   THE ORIGINAL IS $3000
5.  5   FOR I = 1 TO 3
   10   READ R,T
   20   P = 5000
   30   A = P*(1 + R)^T
   40   PRINT ``THE YIELD AT '';R*100;``% FOR
        '';T;``YEARS IS $'';A
   50   NEXT I
   60   DATA .132,3,.12,5,.1075,8

   RUN
   THE YIELD AT 13.2% FOR 3 YEARS IS $7252.85985
   THE YIELD AT 12% FOR 5 YEARS IS
   $8811.70842
   THE YIELD AT 10.75% FOR 8 YEARS IS
   $11316.7021
6.  5   FOR I = 1 TO 3
   10   READ R,T
   20   P = 5000
   30   A = P*(1 + R)^T
   40   PRINT ``THE YIELD AT'';R*100;``% FOR
        '';T;``YEARS IS $'';A
   50   NEXT I
   60   DATA .132,6,.12,10,.1075,16

   RUN
   THE YIELD AT 13.2% FOR 6 YEARS IS $10520.7952
   THE YIELD AT 12% FOR 10 YEARS IS $15529.2411
   THE YIELD AT 10.75% FOR 16 YEARS IS
   $25613.5493
```

BASIC COMPUTER PROJECT 19

EXERCISES

```
1. 20  ?``DEGREES'',``SINE'',``RADIANS''
   50  ?D,SIN(D*R),D*R
2. 20  ?``DEGREES'',``TANGENT'',
       ``RADIANS''
   50  D,TAN(D*R),D*R
```

ON YOUR OWN

```
1. 10  PRINT ``DEGREES'',``SINE'',
       ``COSINE''
   20  LET R = 3.14159/180
   30  FOR D = 10 TO 100 STEP 10
   40  PRINT D,SIN(D*R),COS(D*R)
   50  NEXT D

   RUN
   DEGREES  SINE        COSINE
   10       .173648033  .984807779

   ...      ...         ...
   100      .984808009  -.173646727
```

```
2. 10  PRINT ``DEGREES'',``TANGENT''
   20  LET R = 3.14159/180
   30  FOR D = 10 TO 180 STEP 10
   40  PRINT D,TAN(D*R)
   50  NEXT D

   RUN
   DEGREES  TANGENT
   10       .176326829

   ...      ...
   180      -2.65227048E-06
3. 10  LET A = 45:C = 90:SC = 20
   20  LET B = C-A
   30  LET R = 3.14159/180
   40  LET SA = SC*SIN(A*R)
   50  PRINT ``B = '';B
   60  PRINT ``SA = '';SA

   RUN
   B = 45
   SA = 14.1421263
4. 10  READ A,C,SC
   20  DATA 65,90,30,89,90,60
   30  LET B = C-A
   40  LET R = 3.14159/180
   50  LET SB = SC*SIN(B*R)
   55  LET SA = SC*SIN(A*R)
   60  PRINT ``B = '';B
   70  PRINT ``SA = '';SA
   75  PRINT ``SB = '';SB
   80  GOTO 10

   RUN
   B = 25
   SA = 27.1892215
   SB = 12.6785378
   B = 1
   SA = 59.9908603
   SB = 1.0471435
5. 10  PRINT ``TYPE THE MEASURE OF ANY ANGLE
       OF A RIGHT TRIANGLE''
   20  INPUT A
   30  LET R = 3.14159/180
   40  LET S = SIN(A*R)
   50  LET C = COS(A*R)
   60  LET T = TAN(A*R)
   70  PRINT ``SIN A = '';S
   80  PRINT ``COS A = '';C
   90  PRINT ``TAN A = '';T

   RUN
   TYPE THE MEASURE OF ANY ANGLE OF A RIGHT
   TRIANGLE
   ?60
   SIN A = .866024961
   COS A = .500000766
   TAN A = 1.73204727
6. 10  INPUT ``ANGLE'';A
   20  INPUT ``LENGTH OF SIDE A'';SA
   30  B = 90-A
   40  R = 3.14159/180
   50  SB = 25/TAN(A*R)
   60  SC = 25/SIN(A*R)
   70  PRINT ``B = '';B
   80  PRINT ``SB = '';SB
   90  PRINT ``SC = '';SC
   100 GOTO 10

   RUN
   ANGLE 30
   LENGTH OF SIDE A 5
   B = 60
   SB = 43.3013161
   SC = 50.0000403
```

BASIC COMPUTER PROJECT 20

EXERCISES

1. 15   LET S = 8
2. Line 110 separates each trial.

ON YOUR OWN

```
1. 10    REM COIN SIMULATION
   15    REM ``1'' REPRESENTS H
   17    REM ``2'' REPRESENTS T
   20    PRINT ``HOW MANY TIMES TO TOSS
         COIN?''
   30    INPUT N
   40    PRINT ``HOW MANY TRIALS?''
   50    INPUT T
   60    FOR J = 1 TO T
   70    FOR I = 1 TO N
   80    F = INT(2*RND(1) + 1)
   90    PRINT F
   100   NEXT I
   105   PRINT
   110   NEXT J
   120   END
```

```
2. 10    FOR X = 1 TO 20
   20    F = INT(30*RND(1) + 1)
   30    PRINT F
   40    NEXT X
   50    END
```

```
3. 10    FOR X = 1 TO 20
   20    F = INT(21*RND(1) + 10)
   30    PRINT F
   40    NEXT X
   50    END
```

```
4. 10    REM ``1'' REPRESENTS A GIRL
   15    REM ``2'' REPRESENTS A BOY
   20    LET N = 4
   30    LET T = 20
   60    FOR J = 1 TO T
   70    FOR I = 1 TO N
   80    F = INT(2*RND(1) + 1)
   90    PRINT F
   100   NEXT I
   105   PRINT
   110   NEXT J
   120   END
```